THE

Quality Improvement Field Guide

Achieving and Maintaining Value in Your Organization

THE
Quality Improvement Field Guide

Achieving and Maintaining Value in Your Organization

Matthew A. Barsalou

CRC Press
Taylor & Francis Group
Boca Raton   London   New York

CRC Press is an imprint of the
Taylor & Francis Group, an **informa** business

A PRODUCTIVITY PRESS BOOK

CRC Press
Taylor & Francis Group
6000 Broken Sound Parkway NW, Suite 300
Boca Raton, FL 33487-2742

© 2016 by Taylor & Francis Group, LLC
CRC Press is an imprint of Taylor & Francis Group, an Informa business

No claim to original U.S. Government works

Printed on acid-free paper
Version Date: 20151006

International Standard Book Number-13: 978-1-4987-4574-1 (Paperback)

Visit the Taylor & Francis Web site at
http://www.taylorandfrancis.com

and the CRC Press Web site at
http://www.crcpress.com

Dedicated to the memory of Anna Witkopp

Contents

Preface

The Quality Improvement Field Guide: Achieving and Maintaining Value in Your Organization is intended to serve as both a guide and a quick reference for those new to the field of quality and experienced quality professionals who need a quick overview of an area that they may never have been involved in. Those who are starting their career in quality and those who have suddenly switched to quality will also find it useful. This book covers the many diverse aspects that a quality professional should know to attain mastery in the field of quality.

Even highly specialized quality professionals should understand the field in which they work to be a true professional. This understanding includes the origins of the field and the individuals that have played key roles in the development of the field. They should also understand the many different positions in quality such as the quality engineer and quality technician.

They should also be capable of understanding the many diverse concepts in the field. It would be awkward for an experienced quality manager to have to admit to the customer that their company does not use an 8D report and they have never heard of one. After reading this book, such a quality professional will both know what an 8D report is and have sufficient understanding to correctly use one. The same applies to the many other concepts presented here, such as quality management, FMEAs, and SPC.

Acknowledgments

I would like to thank Mahr Federal Inc. (www.mahr.com) for granting me permission to use their photos of measuring devices.

Note: Integrated Enterprise Excellence and IEE are registered service marks of Smarter Solutions, Inc. In implementing these methods, you are authorized to refer to these marks in a manner that is consistent with the standards set forth herein by Smarter Solutions, Inc., but any and all use of the marks shall insure sole benefit of Smarter Solutions, Inc.

Introduction

Chapter 1 presents a brief history of the field of quality, including the quality gurus' key concepts. The chapter then describes typical positions in the field of quality. Chapter 2 covers the many aspects of quality management. This includes the necessary quality documents such as the quality manual, which includes the quality policy, work instructions, and process instructions. Additional concepts such as computer-aided quality, audits, and training are also discussed. The chapter ends with a description of key quality standards, including ISO 9001:2008, the upcoming ISO 9001:2015, and ISO 9004:2008.

Chapter 3 is dedicated to quality deployment concepts such as capturing the voice of the customer, the Kano model, quality function deployment, and quality policy deployment. The use of SMART goals, SWAT analysis, and key process indicators is also discussed. Chapter 4 covers the seven classic quality tools and the seven new management and planning tools. The seven classic tools are the flowchart, Ishikawa diagram, Pareto diagram, scatter diagram, histogram, check sheet, and run chart. The seven new management and planning tools are the affinity diagram, tree diagram, process decision program chart, matrix diagram, prioritization matrix, interrelationship digraph, and activity network diagram.

Chapter 5 presents methods for failure prevention and detection. These include failure modes and effects analysis for preventing failures, control plan for failure detection, and production part approval process for reporting on preproduction parts and advanced product quality planning. In Chapter 6, measurement system analysis and gage repeatability and reproducibility studies and the basics of maintaining a calibration system are explained. Chapter 7 covers statistics for quality control. Here, statistical process control and process capability and performance assessment methods are explained.

The many aspects of continuous quality improvement are explained in Chapter 8. This includes kaizen for quick improvements, using plan-do-check-act for improvement, performing a root cause analysis, and guidance on creating an employee suggestion program for collecting improvement ideas. Poka-yoke, lean, and Five S are also covered. An overview of Six Sigma is provided, including the phases of a Six Sigma project and the various Six Sigma levels, such as Green Belt and Black Belt.

Chapter 9 covers complaints management and describes the use of 8D reports for reporting on failures and the necessary actions. The handling of both customer and supplier complaints are also discussed. Chapter 10 describes the four types of measurement scales and various measuring devices a quality professional may encounter. A glossary is provided containing basic quality-related terminology.

Author

Matthew A. Barsalou is a statistical problem resolution Master Black Belt at BorgWarner Turbo Systems Engineering GmbH in Kirchheimbolanden, Germany. He holds a master of liberal studies from Fort Hays State University, Hays, Kansas, and a master of science in business administration and engineering from Wilhelm Büchner Hochschule Pfungstadt, Germany. His past positions include quality/laboratory technician, quality engineer, and quality manager.

Barsalou's certifications include TÜV quality management representative, quality manager, quality auditor, and ISO/TS 16949 quality auditor, as well as American Society for Quality (ASQ) certifications as quality technician, quality engineer, and Six Sigma Black Belt. Barsalou is certified as a Lean Six Sigma Master Black Belt by Smarter Solutions, Inc.

He is the editor of the ASQ Statistics Division's publication *Statistics Digest* and a frequent contributor to *Quality Digest*, the *Minitab Blog*, and has published in German, American, and British quality journals. Barsalou is author of the books *Root Cause Analysis: A Step-By-Step Guide to Using the Right Tool at the Right Time* (2015, CRC Press: Boca Raton, FL), *Statistics for Six Sigma Black Belts* (2015, Quality Press, Milwaukee, WI), and *The ASQ Pocket Guide to Statistics for Six Sigma Black Belts* (2015, Quality Press, Milwaukee, WI).

Chapter 1

An Introduction to Quality

The ISO 9000:2005 (2005) standard defines quality as the "degree to which a set of inherent characteristics fulfills requirements." Quality experts such as Ishikawa, Juran, Feigenbaum, and Crosby offer other definitions. Ishikawa (1985) defines quality as "satisfying the requirements of customers" and Juran (1988) considers quality to be "fitness for use." Crosby (1980) considers quality to be "conformance to requirements." Feigenbaum (1983) refers to quality as "the total composite product and service characteristics of marketing, engineering, manufacturing, and maintenance through which the product and service in use will meet the expectations of the customer." Quality is meeting both product or service specifications and customer expectations, and this can be achieved by applying quality management, quality assurance, and quality control.

Juran's *A History of Managing for Quality* traces the history of quality back thousands of years (1995); however, it was on May 16, 1924, that Walter Shewhart of Bell Labs introduced the control chart (Juran 1997). Implementation of control charts in industry did not happen overnight, but it could be argued that the modern field of quality was invited on this day. Control charts and other statistical methods would eventually revolutionize the field of quality by moving quality from a reliance on 100% inspection to ensure quality.

1.1 History of Quality

In the 1800s, mass-production efforts were hindered by lack of uniformity so a system of check fixtures and gages were used to ensure that parts conformed to specifications. Henry Ford also used jigs and fixtures when

1

he created the assembly line, and his engineers also simplified operations so that unskilled people could perform them (Hounshell 1984). Around the same time, Fredrick Winslow Taylor studied people working and attempted to simplify operations using scientific management so that jobs could be completed with less skilled workers than what was previously used (Aitken 1985). Ford's production line and Taylor's scientific management led to the world of mass production in which modern quality methods were developed.

The Western Electric Company's Hawthorne plant relied upon inspections to ensure quality in the early 1920s, and Walter Shewhart designed the control chart at Western Electric Company's Bell Labs in 1924. Shewhart's control chart used statistics to determine if a process was producing acceptable parts; however, it took many years until control charts were used throughout the industry. In 1925, the Hawthorne plant formed a committee that created sampling plans for random sampling of parts (Juran 1997), and the Hawthorne plant's sampling plans were used by the U.S. government in a standard called MIL-STD105A.

During the Second World War, the War Production Board organized training in industrial methods of engineers in industry (Juran 2004); however, many companies stopped using statistical methods after the end of the war (Juran 1995). The quality of American goods declined and the Japanese realized they needed better quality to export their products. W. Edwards Deming and Joseph Juran went to Japan in the 1950s to teach quality and many people give them credit for the high quality of Japanese products.

Karou Ihsikawa also contributed to quality in Japan and he started quality circles (Watson 2004), which spread to the west by the 1970s (Robson 1982). In 1967, America had quality circles; and by the mid-1970s, companies reported millions of dollars in savings. Many business magazines wrote about how successful quality circles were and other companies became interested in quality circles (Cole 1999). In the late 1970s and early 1980s, American management was often blaming workers for being lazy and causing poor quality. The managers saw quality circles as a chance to let workers fix quality problems (Juran 2004).

American managers went to Japan to see firsthand how Japanese quality circles worked, but they failed to consider that quality circles were just one part of a bigger picture. In Japan, both managers and engineers worked together with production personnel to address quality problems, and these actions had upper management support. The American managers failed to see the big picture and quality circles in America were ending in failure by the end of the 1980s (Juran 2004).

American industry had difficulties competing with the Japanese in the 1970s because American quality was lower than Japanese quality and this led to a quality crisis in the 1980s. A video documentary called *If Japan Can, Why Can't We?* was shown on American television and it woke American management up to the problems America was having with quality (Butman 1997). Men known as quality gurus started giving American managers quality advice (Phillips-Donaldson 2004).

1.1.1 Quality Gurus

As mentioned previously, quality gurus were "discovered" during the quality crisis of the 1980s. There is no one definition for what constitutes a guru, and it is easy to find massive lists of "quality gurus" on the Internet. The original gurus were the highly experienced quality professionals who came to the industry's attention during the quality crisis. These men were W. Edwards Deming, Armond Feigenbaum, Phil Crosby, and Joseph Juran. Although he had passed anyway by the time the crisis hit, Walter A. Shewhart also deserves to be mentioned with the other gurus, as well as Karou Ishikawa who gave us so many useful tools.

1.1.1.1 W. Edwards Deming

Dr. W. Edwards Deming has been credited as being the man who brought quality to Japan. It can be argued that such praise is an exaggeration; however, it would be difficult to disregard Deming's many contributions to the quality field. Deming was a statistician who was heavily influenced by Walter Shewhart's statistical process control. Deming went to Japan after the Second World War to use statistical methods in a census. While in Japan, he lectured Japanese engineers and industry leaders on quality and was, without a doubt, highly influential in Japan. He was less influential in America until Japanese industry started to outperform American industries and Americans turned to Deming for help.

He published books such as *The New Economics: For Industry, Government, Education* (1994) and *Out of the Crisis* (1989) where he introduced concepts such as his system of profound knowledge and his fourteen points for management. Deming's (1989) first point calls for a consistency of purpose in improving products and services. This means management must be concerned about both the short-term and long-term survival of a company. Deming was no fan of the pursuit of short-term profits at the expense of a company's long-term survival.

The second point requires the adoption of a new philosophy; the world had changed and was no longer a seller's market, the days of customers buying any product were over, and today quality is needed to attract and maintain customers. With his third point, Deming demanded an end to depending on mass inspection to ensure quality; quality should be built into a product and ensured through statistical methods. Deming's fourth point advised managers to stop selecting suppliers on the basis of price alone; the lowest price supplier may not be the cheapest when quality costs are factored in.

Point five called for constantly improving the system that produces the product or service. This emphasis on continuous improvement is required for a company to survive in today's global market place. Also required is training, which Deming calls for in his sixth point. A trained workforce is essential for achieving a quality product or service. Deming's seventh point required the implementation of leadership; managers should understand their employee's jobs and he expected managers to be able to get assistance from upper management whenever anything happened beyond their control.

Deming's eight point called for eliminating fear from the workplace; employees may be hesitant to report problems if they fear it may cost them their job such as when fixing the problem results in failing to fill a quota. The ninth point demands the elimination of barriers between departments; for example, service personnel should be able to inform the design department if most service calls are due to design issues. Point ten demands the removal of slogans; Deming knew that simply reminding workers to produce a quality product is not the proper way to achieve a quality product.

Deming opposed quotas with his eleventh point. Forcing employees to complete a certain number of parts per hour may result in the number of required parts; however, this may not leave time for dealing with quality problems that might arise. This fits with the twelfth point that required the removal of barriers to taking pride in one's work. The thirteenth point calls for self-improvement for everybody; this fits well with Deming's demands for employee training. The final point is to take the actions necessary to accomplish the transformation that Deming calls for. Deming believed it was everybody's job to accomplish this transformation.

1.1.1.2 Joseph Juran

Joseph Juran's long career in quality began in the mid-1920s, and he was active in quality until the 1990s. Like Deming, he lectured to the Japanese on quality in the 1950s, and his main publications include *Juran on Quality by Design: The New Steps for Planning Quality into Goods and Services* (1992), *Managerial Breakthrough* (1995) and the massive quality tome *Juran's Quality Control Handbook* (Juran and De Feo 2010).

Juran is well-known for his quality trilogy, which is used to provide a way of thinking about quality for all departments, levels, and types of products. Juran called the three points "the concept of the quality trilogy"; however, the trilogy is now called "the Juran trilogy." The Juran trilogy calls for quality planning, control, and improvement. Quality planning requires identifying internal and external customers, determining the needs of the customer, developing products that meet the customer's needs at minimum cost, and developing a process that is capable of producing the needed features. Quality control requires determining what needs to be controlled and how to control it, finding units for measuring what must be controlled and comparing the results to the expected results and taking corrective actions when there is a deviation. Quality improvement is determining what needs improving and how to improve it as well as finding causes and implementing solutions (1986).

1.1.1.3 Karou Ishikawa

Karou Ishikawa was heavily involved in the Japanese quality movement and has been called "the prime mover of quality in Japan" (Watson 2004). He encouraged training for quality in Japanese industry and published methods for achieving quality in journals intended for foremen and production workers. A collection of his tools and methods were published in English as *Guide to Quality Control* (1991). Ishikawa provided practical tools for engineers, foremen, and production personnel, unlike other gurus who often addressed management. Ishikawa believed that quality control is more than just inspection, otherwise one department needs to:

> stand at the exit and guard it in such a way as to prevent defect products from being shipped. If a quality control program emphasizes the manufacturing process, however, involvement is extended to assembly lines, to subcontractors, and to the divisions of purchasing, production engineering, and marketing (1985).

In *What is Total Quality Control?* (1985) Ishikawa points out the need to put quality ahead of short-term profits because quality leads to long-term profits. He also advocated an orientation from the view of the consumer. In regards to management, he advocated cross-functional management with a participatory style. Ishikawa also advocated using facts and data as well as analyzing the data using statistical methods.

Another important concept from Ishikawa is the idea of the internal customer. It may be obvious that a company delivers a product or service to an external customer; however, the processes used to create the service or product also have internal customers. For example, when a department machines a raw part and then hands it over to an assembly department, the assembly department should be viewed as the machine shop's internal customer. Quality problems that happen during machining can negatively impact the assembly operation.

Ishikawa has also been called "the father of quality circles" (Watson 2004). Quality circles are small volunteer groups inside an organization that get together to work in quality improvement. Quality circles are intended to improve an organization as well as use people's full potential and help build respect for humanity (Ishikawa 1985). Quality circles spread from Japan to America but did not deliver the same results as in Japan. The Japanese quality circles were part of a bigger picture and involved higher level engineers and managers than in America. The number of quality circles in America increased in the early 1980s, and few companies in America were still using quality circles by the 1990s (Juran 2004). Quality circles can still be successful, but only when supported by upper management.

1.1.1.4 Walter A. Shewhart

Walter A. Shewhart was a physicist who worked at Bell Telephone's Western Electric Company. He introduced the world to statistical process control (SPC) with the publication of his book *Economic Control of Quality of Manufactured Product* in 1931 (1980). He originated the idea in the early 1920s at a time when the usual method of controlling industrial products was to check each part to verify that it was not defective. Problems in a process could be detected based on a small sample instead of 100% inspection by switching to the use of SPC.

He also introduced the world to an early version of the concept of "plan-do-check-act" in his book *Statistical Method from the Viewpoint of Quality Control* (1986). His concept of "plan-do-check-act" was later refined and made known through Deming. Shewhart could be considered the father of modern quality.

1.1.1.5 Phil Crosby

Phil Crosby has been credited with getting management interested in quality with the publication of his book *Quality is Free: The Art of Making Quality Certain* (1980). Like Deming, Crosby also offered fourteen points for achieving quality; however, his key concept was zero defects. Crosby argued that workers could eliminate failures if they paid more attention.

In 1961, Crosby was at the Martin Company and involved with the quality of Pershing missiles and his job was in danger because one blew up. The situation got him thinking and he realized that acceptable quality level (AQL) sampling plans that accepted some degree of defects were not good enough when a defect-free part was necessary. There result was his Zero Defects concept, which was implemented at Martin Company and quickly spread to other defense contractors (Crosby 1999).

Phil Crosby introduced the world to his concept of Zero Defects as well as his Four Absolutes of Quality Management. Here, Crosby tells us that preventing a quality problem is better than inspecting to identify problems and zero defects should be the expected quality level. He also believed quality is measured in the financial costs of nonconformance and considered quality to be "conformance to requirements (1980)."

He was also a president of the American Society for Quality and a very successful quality consultant. He started the Quality College in 1979 and trained over 100,000 members of upper management in quality (Johnson 2001), and it was Crosby who introduced many higher level managers to quality. Crosby could both communicate clearly using common words and speak the language of management (Watson 2005). Management talks about money and Crosby got the message out that quality is free, making mistakes is what costs money. Crosby's message should be remembered by anybody attempting to convince management to approve a quality improvement project or initiative; speak in terms of money.

1.1.1.6 Armond Feigenbaum

Armond Feigenbaum published the book *Total Quality Control* (1983) describing how to achieve quality. Feigenbaum introduced the concepts of the cost of quality and the hidden factory in one of the first guide books for the field of quality. The hidden factory is the work performed to correct mistakes that have already been made; he saw this as being the equivalent of a second factory within the first. He also introduced the concept of the costs of quality.

There are four basic costs of quality; prevention, appraisal, and internal and external failures (see Table 1.1). Prevention costs are the costs of preventing failures from occurring. Prevention costs include quality training, improvement projects, and product design reviews. Appraisal costs are the costs of detecting failures such as 100% inspection, statistical process control (SPC), and incoming inspections. Internal failure costs are the costs of failures detected before they reach the customer and include scrapping material, rework defective parts, and the cost to review material. External failure costs are the costs of failures detected by the customer such as customer complaints, sorting at the customer, replacement parts, and warranty costs. An increase in prevention or appraisal costs can reduce internal and external failure costs. However, an increase in prevention costs can also reduce or lower the need for appraisal costs. Prevention costs can be viewed as an investment.

Feigenbaum also introduced the concept of total quality control; the integration of the development, improvement, and maintenance of quality efforts by various departments within a company. This integration permits service, marketing, engineering, and production to combine efforts to achieve customer satisfaction at economic levels. Feigenbaum was the last of the original gurus. He passed away on November 13, 2014 and with his passing there are no more living original gurus.

Table 1.1   The Cost of Quality

Type of Cost	Cost of Quality	Description	Examples
Costs of control	Prevention	Cost of preventing failures	Training, improvement projects, product design reviews, and quality planning
	Appraisal	Cost of detecting failures	100% inspection, SPC, incoming inspections, audits, durability testing, calibration of measuring devices and purchasing measuring devices
Costs of failure	Internal failure	Failures detected within the organization	Scrapping material, rework defective parts, the cost to review failed material, production stoppages, and redesigning parts
	External failure	Cost of failures detected by the customer	Customer complaint costs, sorting at the customer, repair at customer, replacement parts, warranty costs and recalls

1.1.2 Quality Today

Quality is perhaps even more important today, than in the days of the quality crisis. In 1994, an 89-year-old Joseph Juran spoke at a convention for quality professionals, and he explained that we are "living behind quality dikes" that protect us from our technology and service interruptions (Juran 2004).

1.2 Positions within Quality

The field of quality is an active and growing field; it would be reasonable to expect the quality professional to take on new roles in the future. However, there are some basic roles that have been around for a while and can be expected to stick around; these are the quality engineer, reliability engineer, quality manager, quality technician, quality inspector, and quality auditor.

1.2.1 Quality Engineer

A quality engineer is the professional responsible for product quality. The quality engineer may use the principles of quality management as well as quality assurance and quality control. Quality engineers frequently write control plans, perform FMEAs, investigate quality failures, and lead or serve as team members in quality improvement projects. Quality engineers often determine inspection criteria and perform quality audits. They also generate quality reports such as reports on the costs of quality failures. They also implement and monitor SPC.

1.2.2 Reliability Engineer

Reliability engineers ensure the reliability of products or systems through the use of tools such as FMEAs and statistical methods. They perform tests to ensure the long-term reliability of products in the design phase and analyze reports of field failures to find out when and why products or systems are failing. A reliability engineer's objective is to identify ways to design reliability into products. This could mean testing material to failure or deciding upon the life expectancy of a product and testing to ensure that a given percentage of the product meets the requirement. Ideally, all parts and systems would survive far beyond their intended service life; however, designing a part to operate for 30,000 hours when the expected service life is only 1,000 hours could significantly drive up manufacturing costs or even render the product not worth pursuing due to high material costs relative to what customers would be willing to spend. The reliability engineer finds the correct balance to prevent this.

1.2.3 Quality Manager

A quality manager is typically responsible for quality planning and maintaining an organization's quality systems. A quality manager may also engage in quality engineer related activities as well as directing quality department staff such as quality engineers and inspectors. Often, this is the person that is designated as a quality management representative in ISO 9001:2008 certified organizations.

1.2.4 Quality Technician

A quality technician performs basic quality tasks such as testing, inspection, analysis, and auditing under the guidance of a quality manager or quality engineer. Quality technicians often perform root cause analysis of quality failures and should understand basic metrology. Quality technicians may also maintain the calibration system and perform measuring device calibration; although, some companies may have a dedicated calibration technician. This is a typical entry level position in the field of quality. Quality technicians may start their career in production; however, many also have at least an associate degree.

1.2.5 Quality Inspector

A quality inspector inspects products and compares the results to a predetermined criterion. The inspector may reject products and prepare basic inspection reports. A quality inspector position may require a high level of skills and education such as a quality control inspector position in the nuclear industry or could be a low-skilled job such as a final inspector at the end of an assembly line.

1.2.6 Auditor

A quality auditor audits products, processes, and quality systems and compares the results of the audit against a standard or specification. Auditor may either be a full-time position or a function performed by others such as a quality manager auditing a supplier's quality system or a quality technician auditing a product.

Chapter 2

Quality Management

Quality management (QM) is the "coordinated activities to direct and control an organization with regard to quality" (ISO 9000:2005 2005). A functioning quality management system is companywide and process oriented. There are international standards available to provide guidance on implementing a quality management system. Quality management is sometimes referred to as total quality management. Quality management includes documents that define the operations of processes that can have an effect on product quality. An important element of quality management is continuous improvement. This is partially important in the modern, competitive environment where industry leaders can be pushed aside by innovative new companies.

The quality management function directs and coordinates the quality actions within an organization. Quality management controls the quality assurance and quality control functions to achieve product or service quality. Quality management is supported by quality assurance and quality control as illustrated by the Venn diagram in Figure 2.1.

Quality assurance (QA) is the "part of quality management focused on providing confidence that quality requirements will be fulfilled" (ISO 9000:2005 2005). Quality assurance uses methods such as process audits. Other methods include the use of failure modes and effects analysis (FMEA), control plans, and measurement system analysis (MSA). Quality assurance is used to provide confidence that quality related requirements are being met.

Quality control (QC) is the "part of quality management focused on fulfilling quality requirements" (ISO 9000:2000 2000). Controlling for quality includes inspecting the product, whether during production in an in-process

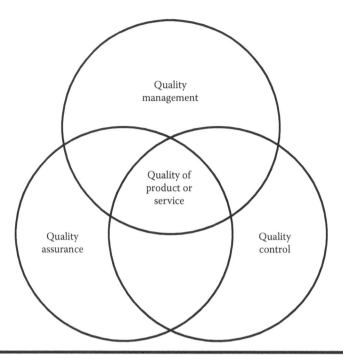

Figure 2.1   QM, QA, and QC.

inspection or as a final inspection as well as the use of statistical process control (SPC), performance testing, and product audits. Quality control ensures that quality requirements are fulfilled.

Quality assurance, quality control, and quality management must be integrated and used together to ensure quality. Statistical process control can send a signal when a process is no longer producing parts in specification; but, it does not matter if the parts are in specification if the wrong parts are being produced. Quality management provides the system that is used to ensure that such mistakes don't happen. Using quality management without quality assurance or quality control is also a mistake because defective parts could be produced even if the processes are functioning properly. For example, tool wear could result in parts being out of specification. The use of inspection as a part of quality control can still play a role in modern quality; inspection may be needed to control the manual assembly of unique products or in situations where there is a danger to life or limb in the event of a failure. However, use of inspection should not be confused with relying purely upon inspection because as Harold F. Dodge warns "you can not [sic] inspect quality into a product" (quoted in Deming 1989).

The quality management, quality assurance, and quality control functions must be integrated to achieve world class quality. The ideal quality system is a system that uses quality management to define the processes that are used and to ensure that the company is producing what the customer wants and needs. Quality assurance is used to ensure that the production system is working properly and quality control ensures that the product is produced in accordance with standards. An example of an integrated quality system would be a mass production company that uses quality management to determine what the customer needs and to ensure that there are clearly defined processes for producing the part. Statistical process control would be used to send a signal to machine operators when the parts are in danger of being out of specification and other quality control methods such as random sampling could be used to further verify the results of the production process. Quality management processes would require corrective actions to be taken based on the results of quality control and quality assurance.

2.1 Quality Management Documents

Quality management documents can be viewed as a hierarchy with less specific high-level requirements and directions at the top and more detailed guidance as one moves down a pyramid. The highest level is the quality manual, followed by process instructions, then work instructions, and finally individual records (see Figure 2.2). The individual records are the various documents in an organization such as measurement reports and test records.

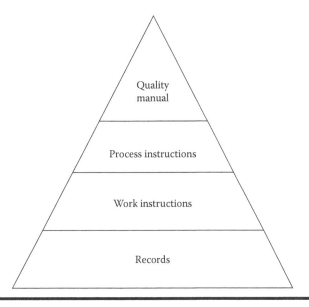

Figure 2.2   Hierarchy of quality documents.

The quality manual may contain both process instructions and work instructions; however, process instructions and work instructions can also be maintained outside of the quality manual. There is only one document that needs to be maintained when the process and work instructions are a part of the quality manual; however, the entire quality manual needs a revision is an individual process or work instruction needs to be updated.

There must be some system for document control. According to Fine and Read, the benefits of document control include keeping documents current, making them available to users, ensuring they are approved by the proper authority, controlling changes and revisions, and archiving older documents. Documents to control include the quality manual, process instructions, work instructions, inspection plans, engineering drawings, and engineering requirements for suppliers (2000). Not all documents in an organization need to be controlled. A document should be controlled if there could be problems if the document is changed such as when a specification on a drawing is changed or a new step is added to a work instruction.

There are many possible ways to store the documents. The simplest approach is to create the documents in a word processer and store them on a central server with printouts in the required locations. The entire manual and supporting instructions can also be printed and stored in designated areas or individual work instructions can be printed so that they are available where they are needed. The location of printouts should be tracked to help ensure that the documents are replaced as soon as a new version is available. The documents can also be stored at an intranet site; however, there is a risk of uncontrolled print copies still used after an update is made. Other storage mediums include in a computer aided quality (CAQ) system or at an html site.

There must be some method of controlling the documents in the quality management system. This can be achieved by using a CAQ program for document management or a spreadsheet as shown in Table 2.1. A spreadsheet is a simple and easy approach to document management; however, this may not be sufficient to meet the needs to a large organization or an organization with multiple locations using the same quality management system. The exact method used must fit the organization.

Table 2.1 List for Controlling Documents

Document Type	Document Number	Document Name	Creation Date	Revision	Revision Date	Description of Revision	Distribution
Process Instruction	PI 1001	Control of documents	February 10, 2014	0		N/A	Qual.
Process Instruction	PI 1002	Control of records	February 10, 2014	1	February 28, 2014	Updated to add sorting checklist	Qual.
Process Instruction	PI 1003	Sales process	February 11, 2014	0		N/A	Sales
Process Instruction	PI 1004	Purchasing process	February 11, 2014	0		N/A	Purch.
Process Instruction	PI 1005	Internal audits	February 11, 2014	0		N/A	Qual.
Process Instruction	PI 1006	External audits	February 11, 2014	0		N/A	Qual.
Process Instruction	PI 1007	Control of nonconforming product	February 11, 2014	0		N/A	Qual., Manuf.
Process Instruction	PI 1008	Corrective actions	February 12, 2014	0		N/A	Qual.
Process Instruction	PI 1009	Prevention actions	February 12, 2014	0		N/A	Qual.

(Continued)

Table 2.1 (*Continued*) List for Controlling Documents

Document Type	Document Number	Document Name	Creation Date	Revision	Revision Date	Description of Revision	Distribution
Process Instruction	PI 1010	Engineering change process	February 12, 2014	0		N/A	Eng.
Work Instruction	WI 1001	Sorting of blocked goods	February 20, 2014	0		N/A	Qual.
Work Instruction	WI 1002	Quarantine of suspect material	February 20, 2014	0		N/A	Qual.
Work Instruction	WI 1003	Milling machine setup	February 24, 2014	0		N/A	Manuf.
Work Instruction	WI 1004	Lathe setup	February 24, 2014	0		N/A	Manuf.
Work Instruction	WI 1005	Inspection machined parts	February 24, 2014	0		N/A	Qual., Manuf.
Work Instruction	WI 1006	Inspection of purchased parts	February 24, 2014	0		N/A	Log., Qual.
Work Instruction	WI 1007	Removal of burrs on machined parts	February 24, 2014	0		N/A	Manuf.

(Continued)

Table 2.1 (*Continued*)   List for Controlling Documents

Document Type	Document Number	Document Name	Creation Date	Revision	Revision Date	Description of Revision	Distribution
Work Instruction	WI 1008	Inspection of machined parts	February 25, 2014	1	February 18, 2015	Use of height gage added	Qual., Manuf.
Work Instruction	WI 1009	Receiving of material	February 25, 2014	0		N/A	Log.
Work Instruction	WI 1010	Shipping of material	February 25, 2014	0		N/A	Log.
Work Instruction	WI 1011	Storing material in warehouse	February 25, 2014	0		N/A	Qual., Manuf., Log.
Work Instruction	WI 1012	Calibration of meas. dev. and gages	February 25, 2014	0		N/A	Qual.
Form	Form 1001	Sorting checklist	February 28, 2014	0		N/A	N/A
Form	Form 1002	Suspect failure report	February 28, 2014	0		N/A	N/A
Form	Form 1003	8D report	February 28, 2014	0		N/A	N/A
Form	Form 1004	Quality notice	February 28, 2014	0		N/A	N/A
Form	Form 1005	Calibration list	February 28, 2014	0		N/A	N/A

2.1.1 Quality Manual

A quality manual can be viewed as an organizations business card. It quickly describes who the organization is and what it does. The exact contents of a quality manual can vary from organization to organization. The quality manual must fit the organization to be effective.

There are specific elements that a quality manual must contain if an organization is registered to a standard that defines what must be in the quality manual. In such situations, the relevant standard should be specified. It can be advantages to have a compliance requirement matrix (CRM) as part of the quality manual if the organization is registered to a standard or seeking registration. The CRM (Chow 2007) both shows where a requirement is addressed and helps to ensure that there are no contradictions such as one procedure contradicting another. A CRM can be created by creating a matrix listing the relevant requirement and part of the standard followed by a description of the requirement. Next to this is the name or number of the relevant procedure followed by a brief description.

It is advisable to have a quality manual even when not required to achieve a registration to a standard. There are certain elements a quality manual should contain even if not required for registration purposes. A basic description of the organization and its history as well as a brief overview of the organization's products or services should be included. The date and version of the quality manual should also be present to help ensure an out of date version is not inadvertently used.

Some quality manuals contain the organization's organizational diagram. The advantage of this is that the people responsible for various roles can be quickly identified. The disadvantage is that the quality manual would need to be updated anytime there is a change in positions. Individual organizations should decide which options are optimal for their needs. Other common elements of quality manuals include procedures for ensuring processes capability, facilities maintenance, calibration of measuring devices, quality data collection and analysis, and employee training and auditing (De Feo and Juran 2014). These items can be in the quality manual or separate documents such as process and work instructions.

A quality manual should also contain the company's quality policy. The quality policy is a high level view and does not specify how the policy will be implemented. It "should summarize the organization's view on the definition of quality, the importance of quality, quality competitiveness, customer relations, internal customer, workforce involvement, quality improvement, planning and organization, and additional subject matter as required" (Westcott 2014).

A quality manual may condition additional company specific information such as the company's vision and mission statement. The vision is what the organizations seek to achieve. The mission statement is a brief explanation of what the organization exists to do. The vision and mission statement should both fit the organization and be visible in what the company does. The organization's key processes should reflect the vision.

Some organizations distribute the quality manual to customers. This provides the customer a quick overview of the organization. It also communicates the company's quality policy to the customer. Such quality manuals may be printed as high-quality brochures. Other organizations may include their processes and work instructions and restrict access to the quality manual due to the proprietary information it may contain. Figure 2.3 shows an example of the table of contents for a quality manual.

2.1.2 Work Instructions

Work (Borrer 2009) instructions provide detailed guidance to those who need to carry out a task. There are variations on work instructions such as setup instructions listing machine parameters for machine setup and assembly instructions contain instructions for assembly operations. Regardless of the type of work instructions, the instructions should be clear and should contain illustrations or photos. An example of a work instruction can be seen in Figure 2.4.

Work instructions should be sufficiently detailed to permit somebody to accomplish the described task, not overly detailed and should not contain extraneous information. Hannon and Grossman mentioned a company that had an 18 page procedure for an operation that took only 30 seconds to perform (2011). There is a high risk that such an overly cumbersome work instruction will be ignored.

The level of detail in the work instruction may vary from organization and should be based on the knowledge level of the person following a work instruction as well as the amount of freedom the person has to make decisions. An unskilled production line employee in a position with high turnover will need more details than an engineer. An unskilled employee will also require simpler text than an engineer; although whenever possible, illustrations should be used for both.

Generic Company Inc.		**Quality Manual: Table of Contents**	Page 1 of 27
Written by: J. Edwards	Approved by: J. Jones	Creation Date: 16 August 2008	Version Date: v.03 11 March 2014

Table of Contents	1
Distribution	2
1 Company Overview	3
2 Quality Policy	5
3 Management Responsibilities	6
4 Quality Management	7
5 Production	12
6 Sales and Service	14
7 Purchasing	16
8 Product Design and Developments	17
9 Control of Documents and Records	20
10 Personnel Policy	24
11 Health and Safety	25
12 Environmental Management	26
13 Measurement and Analysis	27
14 Continuous Improvement	30
15 Management Responsibilities	34

Figure 2.3 Quality manual table of contents.

Generic Company Inc.	**Work Instruction 008: Receiving of Material**		Page 1 of 1
Written by: L. Adams	Approved by: T. Sanders	Creation Date: 03 May 2009	Version Date: v.03 27 January 2015

1 Receiving of Material

2 Purpose

The purpose of this work instruction is to describe how to properly receive and store material.

3 Description of the Work

3.1 Receive the Material

Step 1: Place chock blocks under truck wheels and ensure driver exits cab of vehicle before approaching the load.

Step 2: Compare container and seal number with packing list. Do not open the load. Notify supervisor if there is a discrepancy.

Step 3: Carefully unload the material.

Step 4: Ensure the part quantity listed matches the number of parts on the shipping papers. Notify a supervisor if there is a discrepancy.

From	To	
Machining Inc.	Gen. Co. Inc.	‖‖‖‖‖‖‖

Del. Number	Material Code	Quantity
633819532	847B	12

Part Number	
34856247	

Part Name	Packing Date 2015-01-27
Backplate	Gross Weight 9 KG

ERP Number	Serial Number
2112448	2014 52681

Step 5: Sign for the delivery if the paperwork is in order and part quantity matches.

3.2 FIFO

Step 1: Check the packaging date on the box.

Step 2: Move to the unsorted material holding area and place behind the older material with the same part number.

4.0 Storage of Documents

Place the shipping documents in the proper file.

Figure 2.4   Work instruction.

A work instruction should not be written in an office and then simply handed to the person who will need to follow it. A representative of the people who will use the work instruction should be present when it is created or at least have a chance to review it before it is implemented. An alternative would be to interview represented employees before creating the work instruction. The work instruction should also be field tested prior to release to ensure that it correctly described the operation.

Information such as the creation and version date should be in the work instruction. The name of the person who created the work instruction should also be listed as well as the person who approved the document. The reviewer who approves the document should be a member of the department the document pertains to. For example, a quality engineer may consult with production employees to create a work instruction for a manufacturing process, but the production manager or a supervisor from manufacturing should be the one to give approval. The purpose of the work instruction should be explained. The steps necessary to perform the operation should then be explained. Necessary tools or protective equipment can also be listed if they are necessary for the operation.

2.1.3 Process Instructions

Process instructions describe a high-level view of how a process must function. Process instructions are sometimes called procedures or standard operating procedures (SOPs) and are less specific than work instructions. A process instruction does not define the step-by-step operations needed to complete the processes; instead, it describes what the process must do and who must do it. Like work instructions, the process instruction should include the name or the people who created and approved it as well as a description of the purpose of the process instruction. Generally, there will be more work instructions than process instructions. See Figure 2.5 for an example of a process instruction.

2.2 Audits

Audits are performed to compare a system, process, or product to a standard or specification. This can consist of ensuring a quality management system is in conformance with a certification standard, comparing a process to a process description, making sure production operators work per work instructions, or comparing a finished product to the product's drawing.

Generic Company Inc.	**Process Instruction 005:** Inspection of Product		Page 1 of 1
Written by: B. Smith	Approved by: J. Jones	Creation Date: 18 August 2009	Version Date: v.04 27 June 2014

1 Inspection of Product

2 Purpose

The purpose of this process description is to describe how inspections will be performed and documented.

3 Description of the Process

3.1 Inspection of Purchased Parts

Purchased parts will be inspected by the quality department upon arrival in the warehouse, unless there is a written quality agreement in place with the supplier which would eliminate the need for inspections. Quality can block parts in the ERP system so that an automatic notice will be sent to quality when the parts arrive and the receiving department will place the parts in a holding area for quality. Quality must check for delivery notices at least twice per day and parts may not wait longer than one full working day for the inspection.

3.2 Inspection of Parts During Manufacturing and Assembly

The first and every tenth part machined will be 100% inspected by the machinist according to the parts inspection plan. If a defect is found, all parts in the work order produced before the defect is discovered, will be red tagged as suspect and will be 100% checked. The finished inspection plan will be turned into quality for scanning and storing in the part's file on the company server. The results will be saved in a file named after the work order number.

The conformity of assembled parts will be verified according to the parts inspection plan. The process is not automatic so all parts will be checked and the results will be turned into the quality department for saving on the company server in a file under the work order number. Quality will be notified if a defect is found and the part will be red tagged a suspect.

3.3 Final Inspection

The finished product will be inspected to ensure it conforms to the work order, all relevant documentation is present according to the work order and to ensure the part is properly packaged and labeled. The results will be recorded on the final inspection plan and the results will be turned into quality for storage on the company server.

Figure 2.5 Process instruction.

The person performing the audit is the auditor and the person or organization being audited is the auditee.

There are ethics aspects that must be considered by potential auditors. Information gained during an audit should be considered confidential and can't be shared (Parsowith 1995). Auditors should also avoid potential conflicts of interest or giving the impression of a conflict of interest. Russell describes potential conflicts of interest for audits (2007):

1. You are being asked to audit something you developed.
2. A close friend or relative works in the area.
3. You are currently doing other work for the department or area being audited.
4. There is bad blood or personality conflict with personnel in the aura to be audited.
5. There has been acceptance of or a promise of a gift having value.
6. You are a previous employee of the department or area to be audited.

An auditor should not be a member of the organizational unit being audited. For example, a member of the sales department should not be auditing the sales process. The same rules can be applied to auditing external organizations. The impartiality of an auditor who receives and expensive gift may be called into question.

An audit can be a first party audit where an organization audits itself, second party audit where an external organization performs an audit such as when a customer audits a supplier. A third party audit is performed by a regulator such as the government or a register such as during an ISO 9001 registration audit. Outside of America, the term certification is often used in place of registration (Arter 2003).

A first party audit may be a quality technician auditing a manufacturing process, a quality manager auditing a company's sales process, or an external consultant contracted to audit within a company. Although an external consultant may not be an employee of the company, the audit is still a first party audit when the consultant is contracted by the company. Reasons for performing an internal audit include ensuring the organization is in conformance with standards and documented process and to check processes for effectiveness as well as to seek improvement opportunities (Phillips 2009).

Some customers perform second party audits to ensure suppliers are in conformance with required specifications and documented processes. A supplier that fails an audit may be a potential quality risk. Audit results also provide customers with a basis for comparing suppliers. The audit results should give the supplier a chance to improve performance.

Third party audits are often conducted for registration purposes. This could be a register auditing an organization that is seeking ISO 9001 or some comparable quality certification. A register may also conduct a surveillance audit to ensure that a registered organization is still in conformance with registration requirements. Arter provides four fundamental rules for auditing (2003):

1. Audits provide information for decisions.
2. Auditors are qualified to perform tasks.
3. Measurements are taken against defined requirements.
4. Conclusions are based on facts.

Decisions based on an audit may include whether or not to grant a registration to a decision to implement improvement actions. Naturally, auditors must have sufficient auditing competencies to fulfill the role of audit. This means they need knowledge of both auditing and some degree of subject knowledge experience in the product or process they are auditing. The auditor does not need to be an expert in the subject, although that would be advantages, but the auditor should have a level of understanding. An experienced auditor from a manufacturing company would have a difficult time properly auditing a pharmaceutical company. Measurements during an audit may pertain to measuring the diameter of a product to compare against a drawing during a product audit or a comparison of a process and a process instruction.

There are three basic types of audits, the system audit, process audit, and product audit. They system audit ensures the quality system is effective and fulfills requirements. The process audit accesses the quality capability of the process, and a product audit ensures a product or service meets the required quality characteristics. The audit conclusions must be based on empirical facts and not opinions; opinions have no place in an audit report.

In addition to the basic three types of audits, there are other variations such as 5S audits conducted to ensure a clean and orderly work area and layered process audits (LPN). An LPN audit is performed by a member of management; this has the added advantage that management must go out on the shop floor and see what is actually going on. The audits check top safety and quality risks and are performed by different layers of management according to a schedule (Sittsamer et al. 2007).

The necessary steps for performing an audit are almost the same for various types of audits, although there may be some variation in the complexity and the details (see Table 2.2). For example, a third party registration audit is far more complex than a first party audit of a production process. The Registration audit would require a review of documents such as the quality manual and various process instructions while the process audit may only need a review of the work instructions.

All audits require some degree of preparation. An appointment must be made for the audit and there should be a preliminary review of documents. For a registration audit, this may include reviewing the quality manual, quality policy, and process instructions. For an audit of a manufacturing process the review may consist of reviewing the work instruction for the process. This information should be used to create an audit questionnaire for the audit.

Table 2.2 Audit Phases and Typical Key Tasks

Phase	Tasks

Preparation	• Make appointment for the audit
	• Preliminary document review
	  • Standards, specifications, and other requirements
	  • Quality manual
	  • Quality policy
	  • Process instructions
	• Prepare audit checklist

Opening meeting	• Introductions • Discuss purpose of audit

Audit	• Review documents
	  • Management review
	  • Work instructions
	  • View processes
	• Verify corrective actions from previous audits
	• Document observations
	  • Collect evidence of observations when possible

Closing meeting	• Discuss audit findings
Audit report	• Document audit findings in audit report • Submit audit report to auditee
Follow-up	• Receive plan for corrective actions (if necessary) • Receive updates on plan till completion

The audit must be based on facts and a comparison to a standard, specification, or some other form of requirement. An auditor can compare the operation of a process to a work instruction, verify the calibration of a measuring device, interview employees, and make observations while conducting the audit. For example, an auditor may notice products stored in a filthy location while on the way to the planned audit area. Physical evidence should be collected whenever possible. For example, an auditor may ask for a photocopy of an out of date work instruction found posted in the work area. Observations should be recorded on an audit questionnaire such as the one in Table 2.3.

A closing meeting should be held after compilation of the audit. Key points should be presented so that the auditee is not surprised by major nonconformities that are first mentioned in the audit report. The auditee should also be told when to expect a copy of the audit report.

Table 2.3 Audit Questionnaire

Item #	Requirements Description	Requirements	Non conformance	Evidence
1	ISO 9001:2008 5.6 Management review	Management review planned at regular intervals	Last review was held on May 19, 2012	No review documentation available
2	Process instruction 014: Shipping	Procedure require label to have a printing date	Shipping label for part number 565576 for customer XYZ did not have the print date	Shipping label
3	8D report for Complaint # 202156	8D report states training of operator conductor on July 13, 2014	No record of the training being conducted	No documentation available

The audit report should list the names of the people involved and their roles as well as audit findings as well as a description of the evidence of nonconformance. The nonconformance description should be specific such as "Caliper serial number 597 was found on 03 February 2015 with a calibration that expired on 04 March 2014." Whenever possible, a copy of the evidence should be provided. An example of evidence would be a photocopy of an un-updated controlled document found in the work area. The criteria that were violated should also be listed such as a process instruction that was not followed or a registration standard criterion that was violated. The report should be promptly submitted to the auditee.

The auditee must then define an action plan for the implementation of corrective actions if there are nonconformities. This plan should include implementation deadlines and be presented to the auditor. The auditor may choose to check all of the actions or a random sampling of actions during the next audit. If the nonconformities are serious, or there are much nonconformities, then the auditor should plan a follow up visit to verify implementation.

The audit needs to be planned in advance and starts with an opening meeting where the auditor discusses the purpose if the audit with the auditee, the person being audited. The audit then moves into the audited area and the audit check questionnaire is completed. Leading questions must be avoided and the auditor should avoid sounding accusing if nonconformities are observed.

Unless prohibited by a standard, potential problems should be recorded as improvement opportunities if the potential problem is not at the level of a nonconformity but may become one. A standard may have specific requirements that must be followed. Otherwise, categories such as critical nonconformities, nonconformities, and observations can be used to classify what is observed during the audit. Parsowith recommends three levels of deficiencies. Tier 1 is when there is a systematic problem that affects quality and it is not in accordance with a requirement. Tier 2 is less severe, but there is a conflict with a requirement, but it is not systematic. Tier 3 is for issues that are not a part of the quality system, but have room for improvement (2007).

Deviations found during the audit should be written down and presented to the auditee during a closing meeting. A more formal audit report should be submitted within a reasonable time. The auditee needs to respond with the action plan containing the planned actions and when they will be implemented. A re-audit may be necessary, or the auditor may choose to review the action plan items during a future audit. The severity of the deviations should be the determining factor in this decision.

2.3 Training

Quality professionals are often tasked with conducting training. The quality engineer or quality manager is the best qualified to train employees in a new quality concept or process. Training in the use of measuring devices, statistical process control, inspection methods, or process operations may also be necessary. Ideally, a quality professional filling the role of a trainer should attend a train-the-trainer course to learn the basics of training. Any company contemplating a major training initiative should consider train-the-trainer training for the subject matter experts (SMEs) who will be the trainers. Another option is for experienced trainers in the organization to become trainer coaches to help develop new trainers.

Training is not the same as education; education "is the process of acquiring knowledge and information, usually in a formal manner. Education equips learners to acquire new knowledge by teaching them how to think" and "training is the process of acquiring proficiency in some skill or skill set" (Westcott 2014). The training process consists of performing a needs assessment, preparing the training material, conducting the training and documenting the training (see Figure 2.6). The training process is much like a cycle. The training process should be repeated as new skills are needed or as deficiencies are detected.

A training needs assessment should be performed. The objective is to determine areas in which training may be needed. There may also be situations where there is a need for training due to a change such as the introduction of a new policy, process, tool, or method. The target training audience should also be identified. There may be several separate target audiences for the same training subject. For example, the production

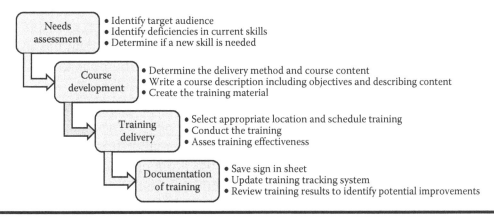

Figure 2.6   The training process.

employees and sales staff may receive different training on the implementation of the same policy.

The method of delivery must be determined. Training material can be delivered as a lecture or as hands-on-training. A combination of the two is also a good possibility. The exact delivery method depends on the type of training and the target audience. Hands-on-training is ideal for a machine operator being trained in a new inspection technique. Members of the purchasing department being trained in a new procedure may be better candidates for lectures.

The training material should be developed based on the type of material, the delivery method, and the target audience. Props and training aids may need to be purchased or made for hands-on examples. Care should be taken if the training material will be delivered using a presentation. Avoid using a font smaller than size 14 so that the material can be easily read by all trainees in the classroom. Limit each slide to four to five bullets points so that the page does not appear cluttered. The use of illustrations is frequently helpful for communicating concepts. The training material should help the trainer to communicate with the trainees and trainers should avoid simply reading from the presentation.

A course description should be written, and it must include the learning objective and a description of the content of the training (see Figure 2.7). The learning objective should reflect the key points and be testable. Training objectives such as "trainees will know how to complete an order" or "learn to place orders correctly" are not specific enough to be testable. Better options would be "trainees will be able to complete an order" or "learners will be capable of describing how to correctly place an order." Training objective should be phrased as some form of action that can be evaluated against a standard.

Trainers need to arrive at the training location early enough to ensure everything is set up and ready to go before the start of training. The appropriate attire for a trainer varies by target audience and industry. The appropriate clothing for teaching production employees will be less formal than the attire required for teaching a room full of executives. A rule of thumb is to dress one level above that of the target audience. A trainer should wear a polo, button down shirt, or blouse if teaching employees wear t-shirts. The trainer should wear business formal if the trainees are dressed business casual.

According to Wrestler, the acronym "FEAR" describes tips for effective training. "Feed" the trainees, "engage" the trainees, and consider the "ambiance" and "repeat"; Wrestler recommends arranging for pizza for the trainees (2014); however, cookies, coffee, tea, and soft drinks should be considered for shorter training sessions. The trainer should also seek

```
┌─────────────────────────────────────────────────┐
│ Course Description                               │
├─────────────────────────────────────────────────┤
│ Subject of Training                              │
│ Use of Digital Calipers                          │
│                                                  │
│ Training Objectives                              │
│ • Trainees will be able to                       │
│   • Correctly measure a machined block           │
│   • Describe significant digits                  │
│   • Zero a caliper                               │
│   • Identify an out of date calibration sticker  │
│                                                  │
│ Course Content                                   │
│ • Measuring machined surfaces with digital calipers │
│ • Significant digits on digital calipers         │
│ • Proper care and use of digital calipers        │
│ • Interpreting calibration stickers              │
│                                                  │
│ Duration of Training                             │
│ 1 hour                                           │
│                                                  │
│ Equipment and Training Aids                      │
│ • Digital calipers                               │
│ • Eight machined blocks with different widths    │
│ • Data collection sheets                         │
└─────────────────────────────────────────────────┘
```

Figure 2.7   Course description.

to engage the trainees; adult learners may quickly lose interest if they are forced to sit through a dry lecture. An effective trainer uses actual situations to illustrate the practical applications of points that are covered in training. Asking the trainees to describe similar situations may also draw the trainees into the material and help to communicate the points the trainer is making. The setting of the training also matters. An unventilated, overcrowded room with loud noise from outside is not optimal for a good training experience. The training room should be large enough for the number of attendees, be well lit, disturbance free, and should be maintained at a comfortable temperature.

The trainer should also reiterate key points of the training material, ideally using different words. A trainer should always remember the main point of training is knowledge transfer. A trainer is teaching for a specific purpose and must often assist the trainees in comprehending the knowledge being transferred. It is helpful to maintain eye contact with the classroom when lecturing; observe the trainees, and take actions if any appear to be confused.

There should be some form of post training test administered to ensure that learners were indeed learning. The exact nature of the test varies with the type of training conducted. The test should consist of a practical demonstration for skill-based training. Multiple choice or open-ended questions can be used to evaluate training of a more theoretical nature. Mitchell offers additional methods such as observing the trainees, quizzes, projects, case histories, and practical sessions (1998). The important thing is to ensure the trainees learned the material they were supposed to learn.

Training records should be maintained for the trainees. A spreadsheet can be used to track who attended a training session on a specific date. There should be some form of evidence to support the spreadsheet; one option is to save a copy of the sign in sheet and the course description in the employees' training record. The exact method of tracing training should be adjusted to fit the needs of the organization.

2.4 Quality Standards

2.4.1 ISO 9000 Series

The ISO 9000 series of standards are produced by the ISO. ISO is Greek for "equality" and is used as the short form of International Organization for Standardization. The ISO is a federation of national standards bodies that serve together on technical committees that vote on the standards.

The ISO 9000 family of standards consists of ISO 9000, which provides definitions related to quality and quality management as well as ISO 9001, which lists the requirements of a quality management system. ISO 9001 is the only standard of the ISO 9000 series that an origination can be certified to. ISO 9004 offers additional guidance on quality management for organizations that seek guidance in going beyond the ISO 9001 standard; however, it is not possible to be certified to ISO 9004. ISO 19011 provides guidance on the auditing of quality and environmental management systems. ISO 9000:2005 (2005) provides an explanation of the terminology used within the ISO 9000 series of standards.

The four digit number after the semi-colon in the name of an ISO standard is the year of release. For example, ISO 9001:1987 is the first version of the ISO 9001 standard. It was updated with ISO 9001:1994, ISO 9001:2000, and the most recent version is ISO 9001:2013. The 2000 version underwent major changes in response to criticism and the 2008 version was only slightly modified for clarification. The next version will be released in late 2015.

2.4.2 ISO 9001:2008

ISO 9001:2008 is the only part of the ISO 9000 series of standards that an organization can be certified to. To achieve certification and organization must implement a quality management system in accordance with the standard. The organization can do this by using internal personal that are knowledgeable in the standard, training internal personal in the standard, or using the services of an external consultant.

The standard requires a process oriented approach to quality. The quality management system must have a documented quality policy and policy objectives as well as a quality manual (see Table 2.4) and documented procedures for control of documents, control of records, internal audits, control of nonconforming product, as well as documented processes for corrective and preventative actions (see Table 2.5). Naturally, an organization may use additional documented procedures if they meet the needs of the organization. The standard provides basic guidance; additional helpful documents include detailed work instructions, inspection checklists, and process maps. There are also records that must be maintained. These include records documenting the management review, training, requirements reviews,

Table 2.4   Required Documents

Document	Clause
Quality policy	4.2.1a
Quality objectives	4.2.1.a
Quality manual	4.2.1.b

Table 2.5   Required Documented Processes

Documented Process	Clause
Control of documents	4.2.3
Control of records	4.2.4
Internal audit	8.2.2
Control of nonconforming product	8.3
Corrective action	8.5.2
Preventive action	8.5.3

design reviews, supplier evaluation, calibration, internal audits, descriptions and disposition of nonconformities, and records of corrective and prevention actions.

Clauses 1–3 are the introduction and only clauses 4–8 contain requirements (Arter and Russel 2009). The introduction to ISO 9001:2008 specifies that an organization's quality management system will be influenced by the organization's environment and associated risks, the needs, and objectives of the organization, the structure and size of the organization as well as the organization's products and processes (2009). The quality management system should fit the organization and not be purchased as an "off the shelf" package.

There should be a process oriented approach to quality management with an emphasis on understanding and meeting requirements, a consideration of processes in regards to value added, results of process performance, and data driven continuous improvement. Plan-do-check-act is suggested to create objectives to meet customer requirements and organizational policies, implementation of the processes, monitoring and measuring the processes, and taking action to continuously improve the performance of processes. The resulting quality management system should demonstrate an organization's ability to meet customer and regulatory requirements and increase customer satisfaction due to continuous improvement and ensuring that requirements will be met (ISO 9001:2008 2009).

Certification to ISO 9001:2008 requires a documented quality policy and quality objectives, a quality manual as well as documented procedures and records. Documented records are those that the organization determines to be necessary for planning, operation, and control of processes. The quality manual must include the scope of the quality management system and must either contain the documented processes established as part of the quality management system or make a reference to the processes. There must also be a description of the interaction between the processes in the quality management system. A documented procedure for the control of documents is also required. This procedure must describe how procedures are approved, updated, how changes are managed, and how the use of an out-of-date version is avoided. There must also be a documented procedure for the control of records.

Top management must provide and support a quality policy that includes both the organization's commitment to fulfill requirements and a commitment to continuous improvement. Organizations certified to ISO 9001:2008 must have a designated quality management representative who is responsible for the quality system and reports directly to the highest management of the organization. The quality management representative may be an employee of the organization with other duties and responsibilities or an external consultant. This person ensures that the needed processes are implemented and maintained and reports to top management on the performance of the quality management system.

The organization's top management must also regularly review the quality management system. The review must include audit results, feedback from customers, the performance of processes, status of prevention and corrective actions, action items from previous reviews, changes that could affect the quality management system and improvement recommendations. The results of the review must be documented.

The organization must provide the resources required to support the quality management system and to support continuous improvement. Resources include human resources and the training of personnel and providing the needed tools and equipment to meet product requirements. There must also be planning for the realization of products; this planning includes creating the necessary documents and procedures, product evaluation methods, and the creation of records to show conformance to requirements. The customer's requirements must be reviewed and understood and there should be a way for the customer to provide feedback and complaints.

Designs must be reviewed, verified to ensure they meet requirements and validated to ensure they are capable of meeting the intended use. Changes to designs must also be reviewed, verified and validated, and documentation of these actions must be saved. There must be criteria for the evaluation and selection of suppliers and documentation on supplier selection and evaluation must be saved. Purchasing information provided to suppliers must be sufficient to clearly communicate what is needed and actions must be taken to ensure purchased product meets requirements. Products and services must be realized under controlled conditions that mean required information and work instructions must be available, equipment and measuring devices must be available, and there needs to be some form of monitoring and measuring. The service and product realization process must also be validated and if required, there needs to be some form of product tractability. Customer property and the product should be protected; protection of product includes identification, packaging, and storage. Measuring devices must be calibrated or verified and records of calibration need to be maintained.

The performance of the quality management systems needs to be measured, monitored, and the results need to be analyzed to ensure the system is effective. There needs to be some form of assessment of customer satisfaction and internal audits must be performed at regularly scheduled intervals. The organization must have a documented procedure for the audit process and records of audits need to be maintained. Both processes and products must be monitored and measured as well. Corrective actions need to be taken if the process is not meeting requirements, and there must be a documented procedure for the handling of nonconforming product. Ideally, suspect or nonconforming product will be labeled as such and segregated from conforming product to ensure is not accidently delivered.

Data must be collected and analyzed to ensure customer satisfaction; products conform to requirements, supplier performance, and for the detection of trends and opportunities to implement preventative actions. The data collected should be used for the continuous improvement of the quality management system, and there must be a documented procedure for the implementation of corrective and preventive actions. An organization cannot simply register to ISO 9001:2008 and assume that no further actions are needed because the organization is registered.

The ISO 9001:2008 standard is a start and not a final destination. The standard requires continuous improvement and an organization can and should move beyond the basic registration requirements to ensure that the customer receives high quality products or services. An organization can further develop the quality management system on its own or seek guidance from ISO 9004:2009.

2.4.3 ISO 9001:2015

The standard ISO 9001:2008 will be superseded by ISO 9001:2015. The new standard will use the same structure as other standards to make the implementation of multiple standards easier. It will also place an emphasis on the identification and control of risks and top management will be expected to play a greater role in aligning quality policies to business needs. There will also be changes in the terminology used. The new standard will not be available until the end of 2015. Organizations will need to implement the new standard within three years of its publication (Naden 2014).

The 2015 version of ISO 9001 is based on three core concepts; the process orientation of ISO 9001:2008, the plan-do-check-act methodology, and an emphasis on risk to prevent unwanted outcomes (Lazarte 2014). The new standard is still a draft and may be changed before the final release; however, changes from the 2008 version are anticipated. These include removing the requirement for a management representative and changing the requirements for control of documents and control of records to documented information. The standard will also require the identification of all needed processes as well as their inputs, outputs, and the required resources for the processes. Risks to goods and services must also be identified and performance indicators need to be selected (Liebesman 2013).

The terms document, procedure, and record are not used in ISO 9001:2015. The terms are being replaced by documented information; however, the new term includes both procedures and records. This change may be intended to reflect the use of computer systems to store information (Dunmire 2014). The revision is also expected to contain a requirement pertaining to the context of the organization in place of an older clause for the work environment. The context of the organization pertains to both internal and external factors that affect the purpose of the organization and the strategic direction of the organization. The SWOT (strength, weakness, opportunities, threats) method or balanced scorecard should be considered for fulfilling the new requirement (Palmes 2014).

2.4.4 ISO 9004:2009

ISO 9004:2009 (2009) provides additional guidance for organizations that want to improve their quality management system beyond the minimum requirements for ISO 9001:2008. ISO 9004:2009 puts an emphasis on improving an organization to improve both customer satisfaction and product quality. An organization cannot be registered to ISO 9004:2009; however, an organization can benefit by following the guidance laid out by the standard. The ISO 9004:2009 standard provides guidance to assist an organization in achieving sustainability, continuous improvement, performance improvement, and it also offers guidance on performing a self-assessment. Registration to ISO 9001:2008 is not a prerequisite for use of ISO 9004:2009; however, the two standards are compatible and can complement each other.

According to ISO 9004:2009, an organization must meet the needs of interested parting in the long term. Interested parties that must be considered include customers, owner or shareholders, members of the organization, the organization's suppliers, and society. However, the organization's environment is constantly changing so an organization's top management should conduct long-term planning, monitor and analyze the organization's environment, identify interested parties and determine how to meet their expectations, and keep interested parties informed as to the organization's actions and plans. The organization should also create relationships with suppliers that are advantages to both parties to identify risks, create processes to fulfill the organization's strategy, and continuously improve.

To achieve these objectives, the organization needs a strategy and policy that can be turned into measurable objectives and deployed. This requires creating the necessary processes to support the strategy, assessing strategic risks and countering those risks, and providing the necessary resources. The strategy must also be communicated to the organization. The necessary resources to achieve the organization's goals must be identified. These include equipment, material, people and their knowledge, financial resources, infrastructure, and suppliers. Processes must be implemented to monitor and develop these resources. Organizations should also consider applying technological solutions and integrate environmental protection into both the design and development of products and the creation of processes.

The standard recommends a process approach with a process map showing the interdependencies and shared resources of processes. The creation of each process requires planning that considers aspects such as markets, risks, resources, inputs and outputs, and regulatory requirements. Each process should have an assigned press owner, with the needed authority to assess and improve the process.

Top management is responsible for the creation of processes to identify current and future needs of interested parties, perform a SWOT assessment, identify new products, and evaluate markets. Unlike, ISO 9001:2008, top management must also assess the labor market and social and economic trends and even local cultural aspects that may pertain to the organization. The organization's progress toward achieving its objectives needs to be assessed and the standard recommends using risk assessments benchmarking, questionnaires, interviews performance reviews, as well as monitoring product and process characteristics.

Key process indicators (KPIs) need to be established. The KPIs should be both controllable by the organization and essential for the success of the organization. The selected KPIs should be suitable for use in making tactical and strategic decisions. Like ISO 9001:2008, ISO 9004:2009 requires internal audits. However, ISO 9004:2009 also calls for self-assessments to be performed by the organization to assess both strengths and weaknesses. The results of the self-assessment should be used to identify both best practices and improvement opportunities. In addition to self-assessment, an organization should perform benchmarking to improve its performance. Benchmarking can be within an organization, with a competitor, or with unrelated organizations. Top management should analyze and review the information that has been gathered so that improvement opportunities can be identified.

Innovation may be necessary due to changes in an organization's environment. The need for innovation must be identified, processes for innovation need to be created, and resources must be provided to support innovation. Innovation can take many forms such as a product that is changed to meet a customer's new need or a new process that results in less variation than the previous process. Both the structure and management system of an organization can be changed as a result of innovation. The organization must also assess the risks associated with innovation.

The appendix to ISO 9004:2009 provides a tool for assessing the performance of the organizational in regards to fulfilling clauses 4–9 of the standard. The organization is evaluated using an organizational maturity model with a scale of 1–5 with 5 being the best result. The appendix contains a questionnaire where the organization can match its current situation to a maturity level. The results are then plotted in a radar diagram, and the organization can use this information to seek improvement opportunities.

There is also an appendix describing the eight quality management principles: Customer focus, leadership, involvement of people, process approach, system approach to management, continual improvement, factual approach to decision making, and mutually beneficial supplier relationships. Certification to ISO 9004:2008 is not possible, but failing to apply the eight principles should not be considered an option. These eight principles must be considered by any organization that wishes to stay competitive and remain in business.

2.4.5 Other Quality Management Standards

The automobile industry quality standard is ISO/TS 16949:2009 (2009). Prior to ISO/TS 16949, the automobile industry had multiple quality standards, which meant that suppliers may need multiple quality systems if they are delivering to several original equipment manufacturers (OEM). American OEMs required suppliers to follow the Automotive Industry Action Groups' (AIAG) QS 9000 standard. German OEMs required suppliers to follow the

Verband der Automobilindustrie's (VDA) VDA 6.1 (2000) quality standard and other countries such as France and Italy had their own quality standards. The harmonization resulting for ISO/TS 16949 eliminated the need for meeting multiple standards. The standard ISO/TS 16949 is a supplement to the general quality management standard ISO 9001:2008 (ISO/TS 16949:2009 2009).

The ISO 9001 and automobile industry standards are not the only quality management standards in use. Other industry specific standards include AS 9001 (2009), which is the quality standard for the aerospace industry. TL 9000 (Pompeo 2003) is the quality standard for the telecommunications industry and ISO 13485:2003 (2003) is the quality standard for the medical devices industry.

Chapter 3

Quality Deployment

The quality policy lays out an organization's high-level objectives, but it does not specify how to achieve them; for that, a quality plan is necessary. The quality plan contains the strategic goals necessary to fulfill the vision contained in the quality policy. Both the quality plan and quality goals must align with the overall strategic plans of the organization, and they are deployed throughout the organization so that lower levels of the organization can implement the plans as actionable objectives (Westcott 2013). Juran offers six steps for quality planning (1995):

1. Define the project.
2. Identify the customers—those who will be impacted by the actions we take to complete the project.
3. Discover customer needs.
4. Develop the product—features that respond to customer needs.
5. Develop processes that are able to produce these product features.
6. Develop controls/transfer operations.

The customers need to be identified once the quality plan creation project is started. It is then necessary to determine what the customers want or need and how these wants and needs can be translated into the features of a product. The wants and needs of a customer can be heard by listening to the voice of the customer (VOC). The VOC can be analyzed with the Kano model and can be translated into features and functions using a quality function deployment.

3.1 Voice of the Customer

It is essential to consider the VOC. The VOC should be there to "remind us that we need to be certain we are addressing customer requirements, not purely internal requirements or our idea of what the customer wants" (Kemp 2006). A customer purchasing a household appliance has no interest in whether or not a component is in specification; the customer cares about what the appliance does and how well it does it. Manufacturers must be careful not to concentrate on meeting technical specifications while ignoring the VOC. Although conformance to technical specifications is necessary, the product must also be useful and appealing to the customer. The mix speed on a blender may be exactly centered on the nominal value, but the speed may not be one which the customer needs.

There are many ways to capture the VOC. An analysis of customer complaints is an easy place to start, but complaints only tell part of the story. What about functions that the customer needs, but were never offered? These functions don't exist and can't fail; therefore, they would be absent from complaint data. Customers can be sent a survey or directly interviewed to help capture the VOC. Another option is a workshop where customers use the product and are asked to provide feedback. Benchmarking comparable products and the use of focus groups are other options. The key is to determine what exactly the customer wants.

A customer purchasing a nail may want to connect two pieces of wood together or maybe just a quick way to hang a hat on the wall. The manufacturer of a product may have no idea what the customer needs without taking the time to find out. Is the customer purchasing a nail going to use it for making a shelf that will sit in a living room or a patio deck that will be exposed to many years of harsh weather? The exact technical specification for each intended use is different. Capturing the VOC is the first step in translating the customer's needs into a technical specification aimed at fulfilling that need.

3.2 Kano Model

The Kano model was created in the 1980s by Noriaki Kano and is used to increase customer satisfaction during product development and is often used together with a quality function deployment (Tague 2005). The Kano model provides a graphic method for assessing as wells as meeting and exceeding the customer's needs. The Kano model is displayed in Figure 3.1.

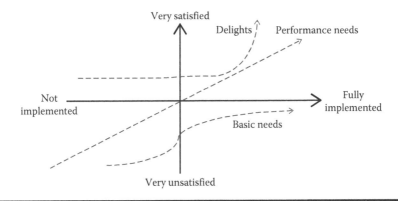

Figure 3.1   Kano model.

The Kano model uses a horizontal and a vertical axis. A product or process that is rated as being at the middle of the vertical axis meets the customer's basic needs, but not anymore. A product or process that is lower along this axis fails, but does not exceed the customer's need. Moving above the middle of the axis leads to exceeding the customer's needs and achieving delight. There are three other lines used in the Kano model. One represents delights; the highpoint of this line is where a need is exceeded and fully implemented. Another line represents performance needs; these are the basic performance requirements that a service or product must achieve. The final line represents basic needs; fulfilling these needs meets the customer's expectations but will not exceed them.

Features that meet basic needs must be present for a customer to be satisfied; however, customers often neglect to state these needs. Excellence in basic needs may go unnoticed by a customer, but failure to meet a basic need will be viewed critically. Delights are above and beyond basic needs, but like basic needs, these may be unexpressed by the customer. Basic needs and delight factors may change over the course of time. For example, in the 1950s a color television set would have a delight factor because color is very nice to have, but not expected. Color televisions were standard in the 1990s and customers would expect to have color without expressing the need; color moved from a delight to a basic need. The same could be said of remote controls for televisions. A remote control was once a delight, but a customer would be very unsatisfied if a new television did not have a remote control.

A product or process must fulfill basic needs to be acceptable to customers. The same product should also offer delights that attract the customer to the product. The horizontal axis shows the degree to which the attributes required to meet the needs are implemented. Those attributes assessed as being on the left side of the axis have not been implanted; those at the far right side have been fully implemented. A positioning at the middle of the axis indicates that the attribute is only partially implemented.

The Kano model is used for creating a product or service; however, it is also relevant for existing products and services. The positioning of a product or service within the Kano model can change over time. For instance, a computer buyer's expectations for memory goes up over time so that a product that may have offered extra memory a few years ago may now be insufficient compared to other computers on the market.

The Kano model is also applicable for the implementation of a quality policy, where the Kano model is used to capture the voice of the customer and translate the customer's wants and needs into actionable characteristics. One way of doing this is the quality function deployment.

3.3 Quality Function Deployment

The quality function deployment (QFD) was created by Yoji Akao in Japan in the 1960s, and it uses the house of quality graphic to analyze the qualities required by the customer, identify the relationship between these qualities, and convert the customer's demand into characteristics and to use this information to develop a design that fulfils the customer's requirements (1990). A QFD provides structure in seeking to translate the needs of the customer into technical specifications.

The graphic used for a QFD is sometimes known as the house of quality because of its house like structure. An example can be seen in Figure 3.2. The house of quality graphic resembles a + with a triangle on top. This triangle is the roof and the reason for the name house of quality.

The left wing of the house of quality lists the customer's wants and needs. These can be based on the customer's stated requirements as well as survey data and other market research. The right wing contains benchmarking data comparing the companies' ability to fulfill these wants and needs against the competitors' products. The middle of the house of quality is the relationship matrix; the ability to fulfill the requirements is listed here, often in the form of symbols representing a numeric evaluation.

Technical factors are listed above the relationship matrix. These are the technical requirements and specifications required to fulfill the requirements. This might, for example, be "closing force not more than 120 N." Above this is the direction of improvement, this usually identified with an arrow that indicates the direction of better quality. If higher closing forces

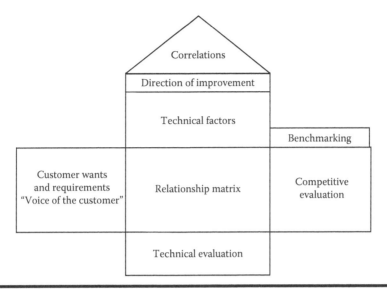

Figure 3.2   House of quality.

are a problem, then the arrow would point down to indicate lower forces are better. The roof of the house of quality shows correlations between requirements. For example, an upper limit to door closing forces may have a negative correlation with a requirement that the door can't easily close without sufficient force. Figure 3.3 shows the elements of a house of quality.

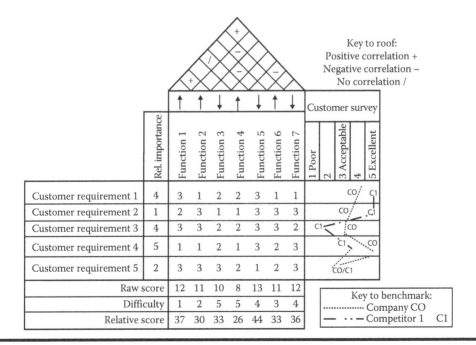

Figure 3.3   House of quality example.

The design requirements identified by the house of quality must be translated into product specifications upon completion of the house of quality. This way the knowledge gained during the QFD can be integrated into the design of the product and customer satisfaction can be achieved.

The translation of customer wants and needs into a product is accomplished by the waterfall model of the QFD. The technical factors identified in the first house of quality are then transferred to the left side of a new house of quality, and the required component characteristics are listed where the technical factors were formerly listed. The new QFD is then completed and a third house of quality is created for the evaluation of process operations as shown in Figure 3.4. A final house of quality is then created to identify the production requirements; these are the actual steps that must be taken during the production process.

The QFD is not limited to product design and manufacturing. It can also be applied to services. The first house of quality is used to translate the voice of the customer into services that will be delivered. The second house of quality is then used to define the characteristics of the service. The third

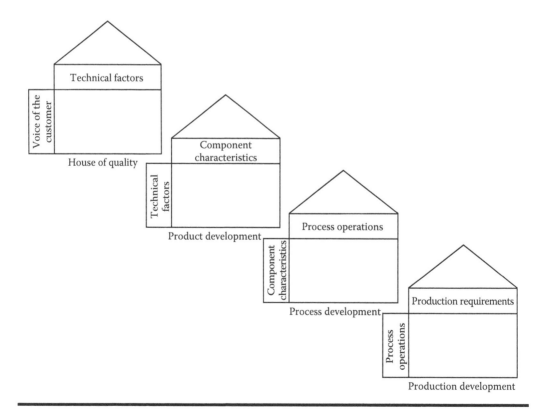

Figure 3.4   Waterfall model of the quality function deployment.

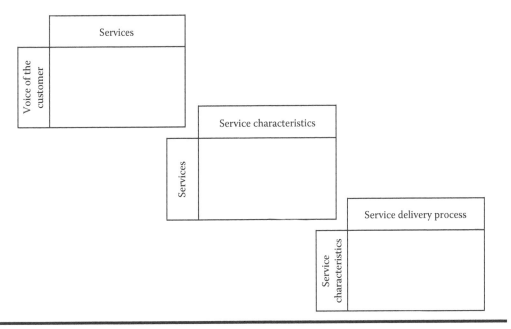

Figure 3.5 Quality function deployment for a service.

house of quality is used for the creation of the service delivery processes (see Figure 3.5). Here, the actual steps necessary to deliver the service to the customer are described and evaluated.

The QFD is also suitable for the development of a quality policy. There are some commonalities between QFDs regardless of whether the QFD is used for a product, service, or policy. The voice of the customer must be captured and evaluated. This is the driving force behind the QFD. A multifunctional team should also be used; however, the exact team members will vary depending upon the intended use of the QFD.

3.4 Quality Policy Deployment

Before deploying a quality policy, an organization must first identify its mission and create a mission statement. A mission is "the reason for the existence of an organization" and the mission statement is "a clear statement of purpose that serves as a guide for strategy and decision making" (Stevenson 1999). A quality policy needs to be created to support the organization's mission. The quality policy serves to guide the organization and may state what the company does and where it wants to be. The quality policy specifies where the organization should go but not how to get there the way a procedure would (Gryna 2001).

An organization should assess its overall situation using a SWOT analysis when creating a quality policy and goals and objectives that support the quality policy. The acronym SWOT stands for "Strength, Weakness, Opportunities and Threats" (Heizer and Render 2001). Strengths can be what the organization does well, or resources the organization can use to achieve a significant advantage. Weaknesses are areas where the organization does not perform as well as it should. Opportunities are possibilities in the organization's environment that can be beneficial to the organization. Threats are external factors that could harm the organization (see Figure 3.6).

The quality policy needs to be translated into a quality plan and deployed throughout the organization. An organization may want to increase market share by 20%, but simply telling every member of the organization, the objective will not translate into implementation. Goals should be set using the acronym SMART: "Specific, Measurable, Agreed upon, Realistic and Time/Cost limited" (Richman 2011). The goal should be clearly described, and there needs to be some way to evaluate the implementation of the goal. Those who must implement it should have some say in the creation of the goal. The goal should also be sufficiently realistic so that it can actually be achieved. There should also be a time frame provided; there should be a deadline for compilation of the objective. Costs are an additional factor that needs to be considered; purchasing a new machine may be a quick way to increase the output of a process, but the machine may be uneconomical.

	Helpful	Harmful
Internal	**Strengths** Currently the market leader for product X	**Weaknesses** High cost of producing product X
External	**Opportunities** Customers are demanding high quality that only we deliver	**Threats** New low cost competitors are entering the market

Figure 3.6 SWOT analysis.

One method of policy deployment is hoshin kanri, also known as hoshin planning. Hoshin planning is based on months of upper level planning and is then implemented over a 5-year period. Quality tools such as affinity diagrams, interrelationship diagraphs, and prioritization matrices are used for visualization during planning. Terminology is also defined so that phrases such as mission, goal, and strategy are clearly understood by everybody. A vision statement is then created to make clear what the organization is expected to do over the next years (Colletti 2013).

Upper management establishes the organization's vision and objectives and then negotiates the necessary goals with middle management. Middle management then negotiates the performance measures, with that will take actions to accomplish the goals. The performance goals monitor the progress made in achieving the organization's goals. These negotiations in hoshin kanri are called "catchball" and multiple rounds of negotiation are necessary. Once the performance measures are established, the teams then have the authority to take the necessary actions to achieve their targets. A hoshin kanri action plan is then created to link the main objectives to individual implementation strategy. An implementation plan is then created to track implementation projects and overall performance is tracked using a hoshin implementation review (Akao 1991).

Whether a strategy is created through hoshin planning or other methods, there must be a plan for implementation of the strategy. De Feo recommends a deployment plan that starts with a vision at the highest level and is then defined as key strategies. Strategic goals are then created based on these key strategies. The strategic goals are then turned into annual goals, which are supported by individual projects (2010) as shown in Figure 3.7. The key strategies should be implemented over a period of 3–5 years, and annual goals should, of course, be completed within 1 year. Individual initiatives and projects may be completed in much less time and they outnumber the annual goals which outnumber the strategic goals.

Strategic goals are divided into multiple annual goals that support the overall strategic goal. These goals are then implemented as projects in various parts of the organization. The high-level projects are, in turn, supported by more concrete projects in lower levels of the organization. Finally, many individual projects are initiated throughout the organization to support higher level goals as depicted in Figure 3.8. An individual process owner can't achieve the strategic goals alone, but they can deliver results that support these goals.

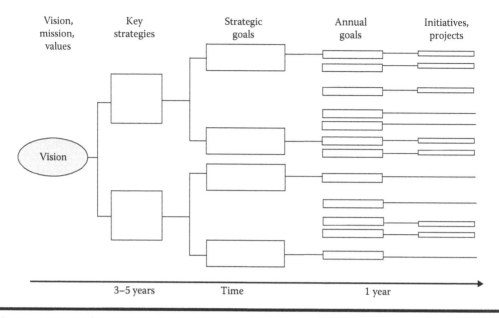

Figure 3.7   Deploying the vision. (Reprinted with permission from Juran Institute, Inc. www.juran.com)

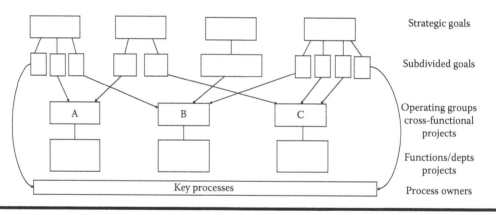

Figure 3.8   Deployment of strategic goals. (Reprinted with permission from Juran Institute, Inc. www.juran.com)

The goals and targets derived from the quality policy should be measurable and support the quality policy. An organization that wants "high quality" should have a multiple lower level goals such as "reduce internal scrap by 15% in the next six months" and "introduce a quality management system by the end of the year." A scrap reduction goal may have multiple projects such as "training machine operators," "install poka-yoke devices at assembly line," and "implementation of SPC for machining operations."

3.5 Key Process Indicators

Key process indicators (KPI) should be identified as the quality policy is being deployed. The KPIs are used to monitor and assess the degree to which organizational objectives have been fulfilled. The selected KPIs must "link strongly to strategic goals and to the vision and mission of the organization" and should "focus on the needs and requirements of internal and external customers" (De Feao and Juran 2014). The purpose of collecting data for KPIs is not data collection; it is to provide management with information to make decisions and take actions, if necessary. The organization should use the KPIs to take actions when there is a danger of an objective not being fulfilled.

The KPIs must be selected to reflect the organizations policy and goals and, therefore, may be specific to the organization. Potential KPIs include inventory on hand, cycle time for inventory, revenue, lead time, employee turnover, scrape rate, customer complaints, supplier complaints, new customer acquisition, customer satisfaction, accounts outstanding, equipment utilization, repair time, and on time delivery.

A KPI reporting format should be created and made available to members of the organization. A large organization may consider making the KPIs available on the organization's intranet site. A smaller organization may simply post spreadsheet based reports on bulletin boards. Reports containing KPIs are often called dashboards, scorecards, or cockpit charts. Figure 3.9 shows a cockpit chart listing five KPIs.

Organizations may opt to use a balanced score card for KPIs. Balanced scorecards consider financial aspects, customer related aspects, internal business processes and learning and growth and provide a balance between short and long-term objectives, financial and non-financial measures, and leading and lagging indicators (Kaplan and Norton 1996). Leading indicators can be used to make a prediction, in contrast to lagging indicators, which only become visible afterwards. The number of orders placed by customers is a leading indicator as it gives an indication as to how material will be sold. Customer complaints are a lagging indicator; failures have already occurred by time the complaint arrives.

A balanced scorecard financial aspect could be revenue growth and a customer aspect could be customer loyalty. A metric for internal processes could be reductions in cycle time and learning and growth could be measured as an increase in training. These aspects have a cause and effect

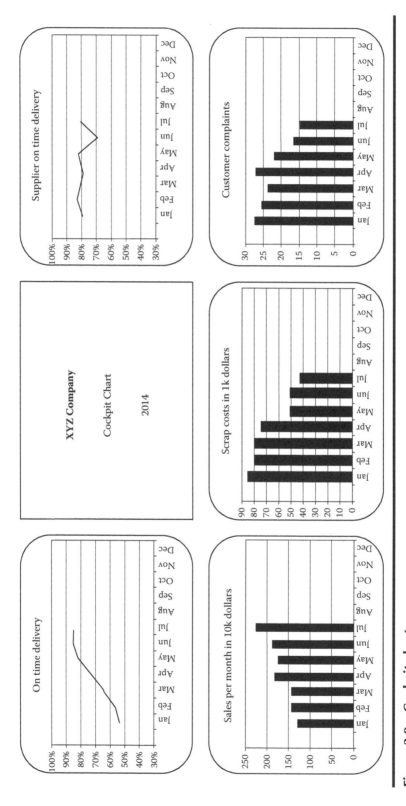

Figure 3.9   Cockpit chart.

relationship, with training resulting in reduced cycle time and customer loyalty increasing due to the reduction in cycle time. An increase in customer loyalty can result in an increase in revenue (Niven 2014). Like other KPI reporting methods, balanced scorecard goals must be translated into measurable metrics. Kaplan and Norton give the example of "number of cooperative engineering efforts" as a measure of customer partnership and "unit cost" as a measure of manufacturing excellence (1992). An example of a balanced scorecard can be viewed in Table 3.1.

Breyfogle offers the Integrated Enterprise Excellence (IEE) performance scorecard as an alternative reporting method. The IEE predictive scorecard uses an individual's control chart and normal probability plot to report performance data as shown in Figure 3.10. The process is assessed for normality to ensure it is predictable; if it is predictable, a predication statement is made. The specification is used when available; otherwise, the median and 80% frequency of occurrence is used. The advantages of IEE performance scorecards include separating common cause from special cause problems, using reporting metrics that are easy for everybody to understand, the ability to identify trends before they become a problem and the ability to measure and quantify improvements (2008).

In addition to KPIs, individual initiatives and process improvement projects should also have some form of metric reported as a process indicator. This makes it possible to assess the effectiveness of improvements. Many routine processes in the organization should also be considered for the implementation of process indicators for reporting. For example, the performance of a process for the assembly of a sub-component can also be measured. Failures that are quickly identified and corrected at this stage of the manufacturing process may not be reported as part of the quality report for the final assembly; but improvement actions may still be necessary at such an early stage in the manufacturing process.

Table 3.1 Example of a Balanced Scorecard

Department Process and Owner	Higher-Level Objective Supported	Balanced Scorecard Category	Metric	Target Level	Actual Level
Change requests (quality engineer)	Compliance in all audits	Internal business process	Requests in progress	<10	3
			Action items in progress	<15	9
			Oldest open request	<30 days	21 days
Budget (manager or leader)	Meet company's expense budget	Financial	Actual vs. planned expenditures	Below budget	Below budget
Performance and staffing (manager or leader)	Complete performance management objectives and development plans on time and use to improve performance	Learning and growth	Objectives submitted on time	100%	100%
			Development plans submitted on time	100%	100%
			Mid-year reviews completed on time	100%	100%
			Significant item on all development plans executed	100%	80%, in progress
			Delinquent training occurrences	0	1
Product development support (quality engineer)	Meet revenue goals and launch schedule for new products	Customer	On-time quality engineering deliverables	90%	97%
			Document turnaround time within three business days	85%	85%

Source: Reprinted with permission from *Quality Progress* © 2011 ASQ, wwww.asq.org

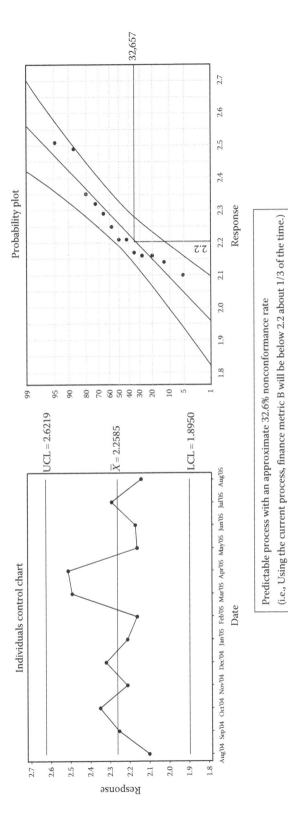

Figure 3.10 IEE performance scorecard. (Reproduced with permission from Integrated Enterprise Excellence Volume II: Business Deployment, Forrest W. Breyfogle III, Citius Publishing, 2008.)

Chapter 4

Quality Tools

There are many tools and methods available to the modern quality practitioner. These tools include the classic seven quality tools, which are flowcharts, Ishikawa diagrams, Pareto diagrams, scatter diagrams, histograms, check sheet, and run chart. There are also the seven new management and planning tools, which are affinity diagrams, tree diagram, process decision program charts, matrix diagrams, prioritization matrices, interrelationship diagraphs, and activity network diagrams. These tools are very versatile and many can be used for root cause analysis, brain storming, prioritizing, and decision making.

4.1 Classic Seven Quality Tools

The classic seven quality tools are seven simple yet highly effective tools often used in the field of quality. Most were brought together by Kaoru Ishikawa for use by Japanese production workers in the 1960s. They were later published in English in a translation of Ishikawa's book *Guide to Quality Control* (1991). They may be known by other names such as "the seven basic tools of quality," "seven basic quality tools," or "the seven quality assurance tools." There is also some disagreement as to which tools are included in the classic seven with stratification sometimes replacing flowcharts. Regardless of what they are called, they are the basic tools of a quality professional.

4.1.1 Flowchart

A flowchart or process map is one of the basic tools of a quality professional, and it is used to graphically represent a process. It could be used
for explaining a process such as in the case of a process instruction,
or it could be used as a tool for mapping an existing process to gain a
better understanding of a process. It also "provides fact-based process
description as a basis for understanding current problems…and opportunities" (George et al. 2005). Each step in the process is listed in a box
with an arrow pointing toward the subsequent process. Decision points
are often represented by a diamond shape such as in the flowchart in
Figure 4.1.

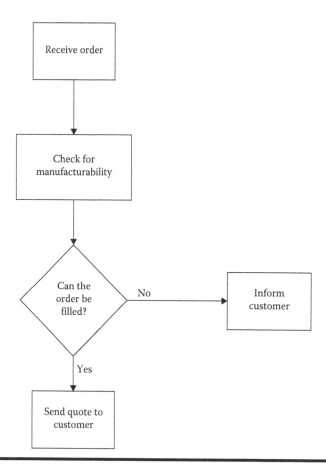

Figure 4.1   Flowchart.

4.1.2 *Ishikawa Diagram*

An Ishikawa diagram, also known as cause and effect diagram or fishbone diagram, is often used for identifying potential influence factors during a root cause analysis. Ishikawa diagrams should not be limited to actual failures; they can also be used for understanding the potential causes of a potential failure. According to Griffith, "The power of a cause and effect diagram is that it forces participants in the problem-solving process (and the brainstorming) to structure the ideas in categories and helps foster new ideas, knowing the categories" (2003).

An Ishikawa diagram consists of the main body with an arrow pointing toward the item under investigation. The lines coming off of the main body are called branches and each branch has additional lines containing twigs. The branches are often based on the six Ms; material, man (people), machine, method, measurements, and milieu (environment). Using an Ishikawa diagram with the six Ms is a good way to begin an RCA when there are many potential causes and the RCA investigation team does not know where to start looking. Using such an approach can lead the investigators deeper into the issue.

Unfortunately, an Ishikawa diagram may become unwieldy once there are too many branches and twigs on the diagram. That makes it difficult to add additional levels of detail so at such a point it may be better to separate the individual branches into separate new Ishikawa diagrams. This makes the Ishikawa diagram easier to understand and permits the addition of new information without unduly cluttering up the Ishikawa diagram.

Figure 4.2 shows an Ishikawa diagram for the investigation of machined cast iron parts found with a loose bolt. Under each of the six Ms is a branch and each branch contains twigs, many of which contain additional information. Adding additional information to the twigs will result in a cluttered diagram that is difficult to interpret, and it may no longer be possible to add new information once all of the available space is used.

In such situations, it may be useful to create additional Ishikawa diagrams based on the original. Here, the branch label becomes the item of interest such as the influence of the cast material on the occurrence of loose bolts. Figure 4.3 contains an Ishikawa diagram based on the material branch of the diagram.

The branch originally named "material" is now the main body and has been better defined with "cast material influences on loose bolt" used for the item under consideration. Three new branches have been created, and

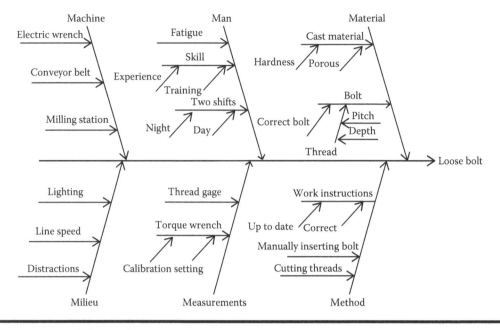

Figure 4.2   Ishikawa diagram.

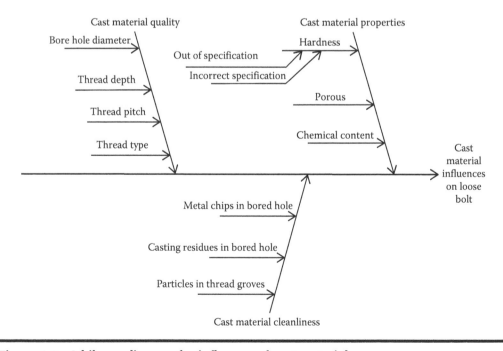

Figure 4.3   Ishikawa diagram for influence of cast material.

there is more space available to add additional information such as the new details added to the hardness twig. The same procedure should be repeated for the other branches of the original Ishikawa diagram.

An Ishikawa diagram for an effect with many potential causes may quickly become cluttered and unwieldy. Splitting the branches into individual diagrams makes modifications easier and permits scaling down in resolution. The six Ms serve as an excellent starting point, but additional diagrams can be added as additional factors coming under consideration.

4.1.3 Pareto Diagram

The Pareto principle was created and misnamed by Joseph Juran who named it after Wilfredo Pareto, an Italian economist who observed that 80% of a country's wealth was owned by just 20% of the people. Juran observed that 80% of quality costs are often caused by 20% of failures. Juran realized that the same principle could be applied to quality with 80% of quality costs are often being caused by 20% of failures. Juran later realized that Pareto's concept was for wealth and the Pareto concept as currently applied originated with Juan himself (Juran 1975). The Pareto diagram is often used when determining priorities between issues.

A Pareto analysis is useful when determining which quality issue should be addressed first. A Pareto analysis could be based on failure types or the costs of failures. For example, to perform a Pareto analysis an analyst must create four columns with the item under investigation on the left side, then the number of occurrences in the column beside it. Add the total number of occurrences and then divide the number of occurrences for an individual item by the total number of occurrences. The number of occurrences for an item divided by the total number of occurrences equals the percentage.

Enter the percentages in the third column. Then add the percentages together in the fourth column to get the cumulative percentages. See Table 4.1 for an example. Use the graphing function of a spreadsheet program to create a Pareto chart as demonstrated in Figure 4.4.

4.1.4 Scatter Diagram

A scatter diagram (Figure 4.5) uses an x and y axes to display the relationships of two variables. The scatter diagram can be used to show possible relationships between the variables on an x and y axes (Tague 2005). Figure 4.5 shows a data set with no correlation between the variables, a positive correlation and

Table 4.1   Pareto Table

Failure	Number of Occurrences	Percentage	Cumulative Percentage
Length	115	81.0	81.0
Diameter	12	8.5	89.5
Scratches	8	5.6	95.1
Rust	4	2.8	97.9
Dirty	3	2.1	100.0

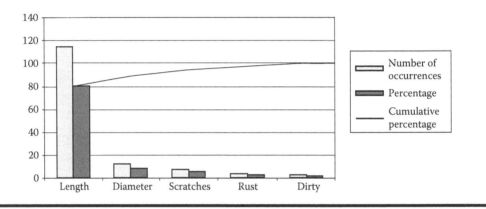

Figure 4.4   Pareto chat.

a negative correlation as well as weak correlations. It is important to remember that correlation is not necessarily causation. A correlation may be found between the price of grain and the price of concrete during the 1980s; however, the causal factor may be an unrelated third variable such as annual inflation.

4.1.5 Histogram

A histogram is a type of bar graph that graphically displays the distribution of a set of data (Ishikawa 1991). A histogram depicts the frequency of occurrences on the y-axis and the measurements for a part on the x-axis. The histogram depicted in Figure 4.6 shows a histogram that is centered on the mean. Data may also be skewed to the left or the right of the mean. Although not a substitute for statistical tests, a histogram can provide a quick indication as to the spread of the data. Normally distributed data can be expected to follow a bell-shaped distribution.

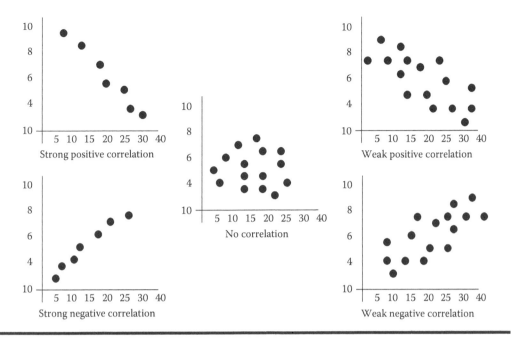

Figure 4.5   Scatter diagrams.

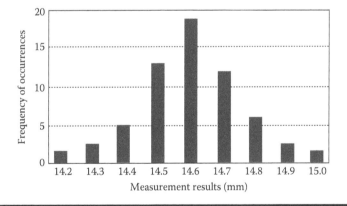

Figure 4.6   Histogram.

4.1.6 Check Sheet

Check sheets are used for collecting data by tallying the number of occurrences of an item. The check sheet in Figure 4.7 shows types of failures on the left, hash marks representing one unit in the middle and the tally on the right hand side. A check sheet can be used to collect data for performing a Pareto analysis or for making a histogram. Typical uses of check sheets include recording defects by type of item, location of defects, and cause of defects (Ishikawa 1991).

Length	⊔⊦⊓ ⊔⊦⊓	‖‖	14
Diameter	⊦⊦⊓ ⊦⊦⊓	⊦⊦⊓ ‖	17
Scratches	⊔⊦⊓ ‖‖		8
Dents	‖‖		3

Figure 4.7   Check sheet.

4.1.7 Run Chart

Run charts are one of the oldest of the classic seven quality tools and are much like a simplified version of statistical process control (SPC). Run charts are used to "track and monitor occurrences over time" (Borrer 2009). The unit under consideration is entered on the *y*-axis. This could be a measurement such as the length of a tube or a quantity such as the number of defects detected. The *x*-axis is the sequence of the data collection. The data may need to be normalized if the number of defects detected is used in cases where the sample size varies. This can easily be done by converting from the absolute number of defective units to a percentage. A run chart can be seen in Figure 4.8.

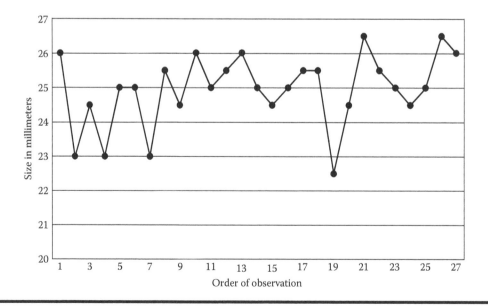

Figure 4.8   Run chart.

4.2 Seven New Management and Planning Tools

In addition to the classic seven quality tools, there are seven new management and planning tools. These tools were brought together as a tool set from many existing tools as a result of Japanese operations research in the 1970s (Brassard 1996). The new tools are intended for use by a team, and they are intended to "promote ways to innovate, communicate, and plan" (Duffy et al. 2012). There are many potential uses for the seven management and planning tools, and the selection of the tool should be based upon what needs to be accomplished.

4.2.1 Affinity Diagram

An affinity diagram is used to identify the main themes pertaining to an issue by logically grouping many concepts (ReVelle 2004). The team members use index cards to write words or phrases related to the problem at hand, and these are then arranged in logical groupings. Often, it will take several tries to find the final arrangement. Each grouping is then given a label that best describes it. The affinity diagram in Figure 4.9 is being used to identify aspects that must be considered when organizing a training session.

4.2.2 Tree Diagram

Using a tree diagram helps you to "move your thinking from generalities to specifics" (Tague 2005). The overall objective is written on the left side of the tree as shown in Figure 4.10. This is then broken down into more

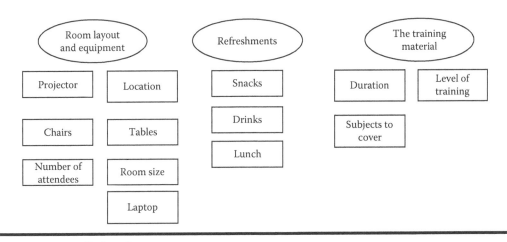

Figure 4.9   Affinity diagram.

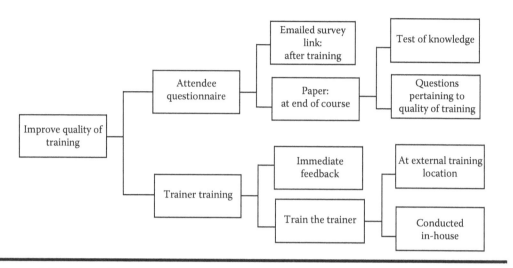

Figure 4.10   Tree diagram.

specific aspects. Each higher level aspect can have one or more lower level aspects. The specific aspects to consider are those listed at the lowest level of the tree. These aspects must be evaluated to fully consider the general aspect at the left side of the tree.

4.2.3 Process Decision Program Chart

The process design program chart (PDPC) is used to map to possible outcomes leading out from a problem statement (Brassard 1996) or a concept that is being evaluated. The PDPC starts with a concept that is being considered at the highest level. In the example in Figure 4.11, the concept is planning to conduct a training class. The concept is listed at the highest level and beneath it are options that are being considered. Tasks necessary to implement these options are listed at the third level. Potential problems that can be encountered are listed at the fourth level and prevention actions are listed as the fifth and final level.

Each option can have more than one task and each task can have more than one potential problem. The levels can be labeled or shapes can be used to differentiate between tasks, risks, and preventative actions.

4.2.4 Matrix Diagram

A matrix diagram shows the relationships between groups of information, and there are many potential shapes available (Tague 2005). The most basic matrix diagram is the L-shaped diagram. The matrix diagram in Table 4.2

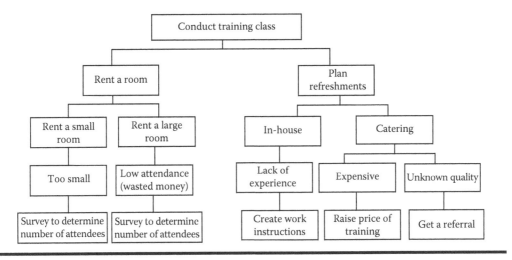

Figure 4.11   Process design program chart.

Table 4.2   Matrix Diagram

	Location 1	*Location 2*	*Location 3*
Central location	Yes	Yes	Yes
Near train station	No	Yes	Yes
Parking available	Yes	Yes	No

shows three requirements that must be considered when selecting a training location. The top of the matrix lists three potential locations where training can be held. The matrix was then used to identify which location fulfilled the requirements.

4.2.5 Prioritization Matrix

A prioritization matrix uses weighted criteria to help when choosing between various options (ReVelle 2004). The prioritization diagram is much like a matrix diagram; however, the requirements being considered are assigned a weighted value, and each option under consideration is then evaluated in terms of how well it fulfills the requirements. The weighted values are then multiplied by the assessed value of the option, and each option column is totaled to determine which option best fulfills all requirements while considering both the degree of fulfillment and the importance of the requirement as shown in Table 4.3.

Table 4.3   Prioritization Matrix

	Weighted Value	*Option 1*	*Option 2*	*Option 3*
Central location	5	6	6	6
Near train station	7	1	6	6
Parking available	7	6	6	1
Costs	8	6	3	1
Catering	10	6	3	6
Total:		187	168	147
%:		74.2	66.7	58.3

Degree of fulfillment: 1, not at all; 3, fair; 6, complete fulfillment.

4.2.6 *Interrelationship Diagraph*

An interrelationship diagraph is the interrelationship between problems of options (Brassard 1996). Factors are first listed on index cards. Then, arrows are added to show which factor is an influence on another factor. The interrelationship diagraph shows which factor has the biggest influence. In Figure 4.12, an unprepared instructor can be seen as the biggest risk to the organization.

4.2.7 *Activity Network Diagram*

An activity network diagram is much like a PERT chart (Kubiak and Benbow 2009). A PERT (Program Evaluation and Review Technique) chart helps to

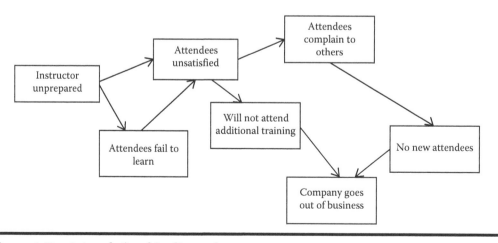

Figure 4.12   Interrelationship diagram.

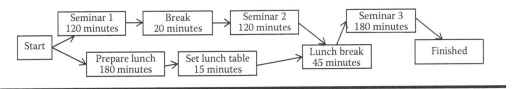

Figure 4.13 Activity network diagram.

identify the critical path, which is the longest path leading to project completion (Kerzner 1998). Individual tasks or operations are listed in the order in which they must occur. The time required to complete the task or operation is also listed and the steps are connected in order by arrows. Figure 4.13 shows tasks that must happen during a training session. The preparation of lunch is conducted in parallel to the training and both sets of operations must be completed before lunch can begin. The training takes a total of 250 minutes to complete and lunch preparation takes only 195 minutes. The training is the critical path; however, lunch will be delayed if lunch preparation starts later than 55 minutes after the start of training.

Chapter 5

Failure Prevention
and Detection

Often, companies seek to improve their products and processes after receiving a customer complaint. Product quality should not be the result of customer complaints; quality should be built into products and processes. The use of failure mode and effects analysis (FMEA) and control plans can help ensure that failed products don't reach customers with the FMEA used for prevention, and the control plan used for detection so that even if a failure occurs, it will not reach the customer. Quality planning can help to ensure the smooth launch of a product or process, and this can be accomplished by the use of advanced quality planning process (APQP).

5.1 Failure Mode and Effects Analysis

A FMEA is used in product development and in the creation of a new process to identify and assess potential failure modes and their severity. There are two main types of typical FMEAs. The design FMEA (DFMEA) is used during the product design phase and process FMEA (PFMEA) is used for the production process (Chrysler et al. 2008b). There are many other types of FMEAs; however, they are all variations of these two basic types. There are many standards describing FMEA forms, and some companies create their own version in a spreadsheet. Figure 5.1 shows an AIAG DFMEA form and Figure 5.2 shows an AIAG PFMEA form. Other forms may differ; however, FMEA forms a generally very similar in both layout and content.

Item / FUNCTION Requirements	Potential Failure Mode	Potential Effects(s) of Failure	Severity	Classification	Potential Cause(s) of Failure	Occurrence	Current Design Controls Prevention	Current Design Controls Detection	Detection	RPN	Recommended Action	Responsibility & Target Completion Date	Actions Taken & Effective Date	Severity	Occurrence	Detection	RPN

POTENTIAL FAILURE MODE AND EFFECTS ANALYSIS (DESIGN FMEA)

System ___ Subsystem ___ Component ___ Model Year(s)/Program(s) ___ Core Team ___

Design Responsibility ___ Key Date ___

FMEA Number ___ Page ___ of ___ Prepared By: ___ FMEA Date (Orig.) ___

Action Results

Figure 5.1 Design FMEA form. (From Chrysler et al., *Potential Failure Modes and Effects Analysis (FMEA)*, 4th edn., Automotive Industry Action Group, United States, 2008b.)

Figure 5.2 **Process FMEA form. (From Chrysler et al., *Potential Failure Modes and Effects Analysis (FMEA)*, 4th edn., Automotive Industry Action Group, United States, 2008b.)**

Regardless of the type of FMEA, there are some commonalities. For example, a cross functional team should be formed with an FMEA moderator responsible for writing and updating the FMEA. The FMEA moderator must be thoroughly familiar with the FMEA methodology. This person serves as a facilitator by providing advice and guiding the team members through the FMEA process. The FMEA team requires members knowledgeable on the product or process that is being evaluated. An FMEA for a product that is moved between departments while being processed will require the support of team members who are knowledgeable in the various processes that will work on the product. Additional support may also be needed. A member of the team should be designated to ensure that the team members carry out assigned tasks such as improvement activates. This is especially important when the tasks are given to somebody outside of the FMEA team.

Information must be collected after an FMEA team is formed. Information sources include old FMEAs for comparable product or processes; quality data including known failures, product drawings, and bill of materials; as well as the customer's operating conditions for a DFMEA. Although older FMEAs are a good source of information, they should not be simply renamed and used for the new product or process. For example, a seal manufacturer producing a seal for a new customer should consider this customer's intended use when creating or updating a DFMEA for the new customer. This customer's intended use may differ from that of previous customers; the new use may entail risks that were not evaluated in previous DFMEAs.

A process flowchart is a critical element in creating a PFMEA as it contains the process steps that are to be evaluated. Each step in the flowchart should be considered for inclusion in the PFMEA. If process steps are named such as "turning operation" or numbered, this information can be entered into the PFMEA form to quickly tie the flowchart to the PFMEA. A process flowchart must be created if one does not already exist. Exiting flowcharts should be verified to ensure that the process has not changed since the last time the flowchart was updated. A visit to the actual process is also advantages when preparing to create a PFMEA.

Useful preparation tools for a DFMEA include the boundary diagram and the parameter diagram. According to the Chrysler, Ford, General Motors Supplier Quality Requirements Task Force, the boundary diagram "shows the physical and logical relationships between the components of the product" (2008). The boundary diagram can be for the individual components in an assembly or system or for the entire systems.

The example in Figure 5.3 depicts a washing machine's interactions with its environment. External inputs into the washing machine include washing detergent, fabric softener, dirty clothes, fresh water, and electricity. Outputs from the washing machine include waste water and clean clothes. The washing machine boundary diagram can be used to identify external influences, which could affect the operation of the washing machine. For example, the machine will fail to function properly if the required electricity deviates outside of a specific range. Fresh water containing large amounts of calcium could result in calcium deposits that clog the washing machine and lead to a degradation in performance.

The parameters diagram "is a structured tool to help the team understand the physics related to the function(s) of the design" (Chrysler et al. 2008b).

Parameter diagrams analyze input factors, noise factors, control factors, ideal functions, and error states. Figure 5.4 shows a parameter diagram for a washing machine. The inputs include the clothes and detergent that are put into the machine. Control factors are the time, temperature, and speed that can be adjusted. Noise factors are influences that can't be controlled. They may be due to variation such as the weight of different loads of laundry, interactions with other systems, changes over time such as the wear of a drive belt, the way in which the customer uses the system, and environmental factors such as water pressure. The ideal state is clean clothes and potential error states include clothes that were not cleaned, clothes that shrunk, and an incomplete rinse cycle.

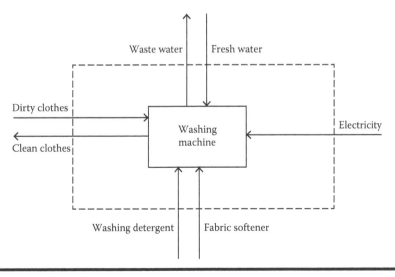

Figure 5.3   Boundary diagram.

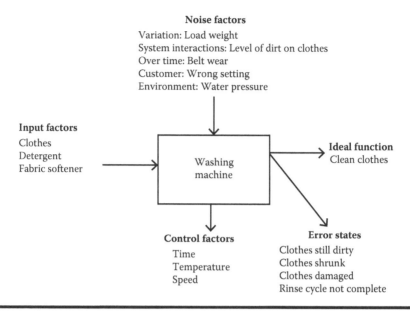

Noise factors
Variation: Load weight
System interactions: Level of dirt on clothes
Over time: Belt wear
Customer: Wrong setting
Environment: Water pressure

Input factors
Clothes
Detergent
Fabric softener

Washing machine

Ideal function
Clean clothes

Control factors
Time
Temperature
Speed

Error states
Clothes still dirty
Clothes shrunk
Clothes damaged
Rinse cycle not complete

Figure 5.4   Parameter diagram.

The boundary diagram and parameter diagram are useful for identifying functions and failures in a DFMEA. For example, the washing machine could be negatively affected by variation in the electricity entering the machine. The resulting failures and effects could then be analyzed in detail in the DFMEA.

Additional quality tools such as Ishikawa diagrams and affinity diagrams may be useful for both DFMEAs and PDMEAs. Such tool can be applied to facilitate brainstorming when considering what could go wrong with a product or process. Proper FMEA preparation can help to ensure that all relevant potential failures are considered in the final FMEA.

The DFMEA and PFMEA differ in the first field of the FMEA form. The first field in the DFMEA form is for the function and the second field is for the requirement. The function is a description of that the design must do and the requirement describes the way it must be done. The process function and requirement is the first field in the PFMEA. The process function is a brief description of the action performed in the process step. The requirement describes the way in which the step is performed. Negations of the requirement are the failure mode.

The potential failure mode describes the way in which the part or process could fail to function properly. For example, a control lever that has the requirement "move freely" could have the failure mode "control lever sticks." The process requirement in a PFMEA could be "drill 0.2 mm hole in control lever" with the failure mode "hole out of tolerance." The failure is the cause of the failure mode. A failure mode for a DFMEA may be "control lever hole tolerance incorrect." The failure mode in the PFMEA may be "drill bit worn." Often, one failure mode will have more than one potential cause.

Every failure must have an effect; the failure effect is the unwanted consequence of the failure occurring. A DFMEA failure effect may be "reduced control" while a PFMEA effect could be "control lever not mountable." A failure effect may lead to additional effects in a chain of failures. These additional effects should be listed with the first effect. A failure mode could have many different possible effects. After listing failures effects, the severity of each failure effect must be evaluated. The severity is the consequence of the failure occurring and is evaluated on a scale of 1–10, with 10 being the worst. Generally, there are tables available to ensure a consistent evaluation.

The current detection and prevention activities are then evaluated. These are the activities that are currently being performed or will be performed. The planned activities for failure prevention are evaluated to determine a score for prevention, which is the subjective estimated chance of detecting a failure that has occurred using a scale of 1–10. Prevention activities are taken to prevent a failure from happening, and there can be multiple actions to prevent one failure. A DFMEA prevention action could be "design per Design Rule 7235a." A prevention activity for a PFMEA could be "replace drill bit after X number of uses." Detection actions are taken to ensure the problem is detected if it does occur. A DFMEA detection action could be "prototype testing" and a PFMEA detection action could be "check hole every 200 parts." Like prevention, there are tables available for the evaluation of detection. Detection activities are also evaluated with tables on a scale of 1–10. Various tables for severity, occurrence, and detection are available such as the one produced by the Automotive Industry Action Group (Chrysler et al. 2008b). Table 5.1 shows generic severity, occurrence, and detection tables.

A risk priority number (RPN) is determined by multiplying severity times occurrence times detection. There should be no one RPN cutoff number; generally, RPNs are used to prioritize and improvements are implemented for the higher RPNs first. The RPN should not overrule common sense; higher combinations of severity and occurrence should be a higher priority than lower severity issues with a higher RPN. In addition to the RPN, the combination of severity and occurrence should also be considered. Many FMEA forms have a field for classification. This field can be used to indicate a high risk items such as when there is a high severity rating or a high combination for severity and occurrence.

Table 5.1   Generic FMEA Tables

Severity Table		Occurrence Table		Detection Table	
Rating	*Severity Description*	*Rating*	*Occurrence Description*	*Rating*	*Detection Description*
10	Safety risk	10	Certain to occur	10	Impossible to detect
8	Property damage	8	Might occur	8	Little chance of detection
6	Complete failure of system	6	Moderate risk of occurrence	6	Might detect
4	Reduced functionality	4	Low risk of occurrence	4	Moderate chance of detection
2	Occasional annoyance	2	Very low risk of occurrence	2	High chance of detection
1	Not noticeable	1	Can't occur	1	Detection is certain

The FMEA form has a place to list improved prevention and detection actions; the moderator should track the status of the actions, and the team should reevaluate items once the improvement actions are implemented. Severity is seldom reduced; improved prevention and detection activities reduce the change of a failure occurring but don't change the consequences of a failure occurring. Severity can only be reduced by using a different design concept that can't have the same failure effect that had the high severity. Occurrence and detection scores can be lowered by successfully implementing additional actions, and the RPN needs to be recalculated after the introduction of improvement actions.

The DFMEA should be started at the beginning of a new design project. The results of the DFMEA can then be used as an input for the creation of the PFMEA. The PFMEA then serves as an input for the creation of a control plan to ensure the necessary inspection actions are carried out.

5.2   Control Plan

Control plans are used to document the way in which parts and processes are controlled at each step of a process (Borrer 2009). Inspection related inputs from the PFMEA should be entered into the control plan to ensure the inspections are carried out. Engineering drawings and product specifications should also be consulted when creating or updating a control plan. Often, the control plan will need to be updated as a result of a customer complaint or the discovery of a new failure. Control plans should also be reviewed when drawings are updated. An example of a control plan form can be seen in Figure 5.5.

Control plans are not only for manufacturing of a product; "the control plan describes the actions that are required at each phase of the process including receiving, in-process, out-going, and periodic requirements to assure that all process outputs will be in a state of control" (Chrysler et al. 2008a). Control plans can also be used for service related processes such as order taking or the delivery of a service such as insurance sales. The exact content and layout of a control plan may vary from company to company; however, some key elements should be present in all control plans. The top of a control plan contains details such as the control plan number, the part name and number, and the current version of the part.

Control plans list the process step, a brief name that describes the process step and the physical location of the process. The characteristic that is to be inspected needs to be described, such as "screw head flush." The characteristic could pertain to attribute data such as the surface appearance of a product or variable data such as a dimension. The characteristic description should help the person doing the inspection to identify exactly what they should check. High risk items can be identified in the special characteristic field.

The specification or tolerance also needs to be listed in the control plan so that the person doing the inspection has clear acceptance and rejection criteria. The evaluation method must also be given. This could be a check with a specific gage, a visual check, or the use of a measuring device. If a gage or measuring device is used, it should be described in sufficient detail to ensure that the correct device is used.

The sample size needs to be listed, and the frequency of inspections needs to be given. This could be once per hour or shift or every 100 parts. The control method needs to be described. This could be simply recording the results on a check sheet or entering the data into an SPC chart. Preplanned actions to take if nonconforming parts are found are listed under the reaction plan. This is intended to give the person doing the inspection guidance on what to do if nonconforming parts are identified. Typical reactions include blocking and checking all parts produced between the failed check and the last check that was passed. Either the quality department or the process owner should be informed if a part failed a check.

CONTROL PLAN

☐ Prototype   ☐ Pre-Launch   ☐ Production   Page 1 of 1

Control Plan Number	Key Contact/Phone	Date (Orig.)	Date (Rev.)
Part Number/Latest Change Level	Core Team		Customer Engineering Approval/Date (If Req'd.)
Part Name/Description	Orgnization/Plant approval Date		Customer Quality Approval/Date Iif Req'd.)
Orginization/Plant Orgnization Code	Other Approval/Date (If Req'd.)		Other Approval/Date (If Req'd)

PART/ PROCESS NUMBER	PROCESS NAME/ OPERTION DESCRIPTION	MACHINE, DEVICE, JIG, TOOLS FOR MFG.	CHARACTERISTICS			SPECIAL CHAR CLASS	PRODUCT/PROCESS SPECIFICATION/ TOLERANCE	METHODS				REACTION PLAN
			NO.	PRODUCT	PROCESS			EVALUATION/ MEASURMENT TECHNIQUE	SAMPLE		CONTROL METHOD	
									SIZE	FREQ.		

Figure 5.5   Control plan. (From Chrysler et al., *Advanced Product Quality Planning and Control Plan: APQP*, 2nd edn., Automotive Industry Action Group, United States, 2008a.)

The completed control plan must be available to those in production who must either carry out the inspections or ensure the inspections are carried out. Control plans serve no purpose if they are not available to the people who will need to use them.

5.3 Production Part Approval Process

The production part approval process (PPAP) is used heavily in the automotive industry when a supplier delivers new parts or components to a customer. The intent is to ensure the supplier has fully understood the customer's requirements for the engineering drawing and specification; it also ensures that the supplier can consistently produce the part at the required quantities (Chrysler et al. 2006).

A PPAP preformed according to AIAG requirements has a part submission warrant (PSW) that summarizes the entire PPAP (see Figure 5.6). The PSW includes details such as the customer and supplier part numbers, drawing number and drawing version, date of engineering changes, tools used for checking the parts, weight of the part, supplier information, information on material used in the part, and the reason for the PPAP submission. Reasons for issuing a PPAP are new parts, changes to existing parts, changes to tooling, corrections to the part, not using the tool within a 1-year period, changes to the design or material of the part, changing suppliers, changes to the production process, the addition of a different production location, or other reasons if needed (Chrysler et al. 2006).

There is a field in the PPAP document for the IMDS (International Material Data System) reporting information. The automotive industry uses the IMDS for tracking the substances used in automotive components. The supplier, or a third-party contractor for the supplier, enters the material into the IMDS, and the automotive manufactures can quickly identify material in components and compare the material to various regulations. Generally, the supplier enters the IMDS reporting number into the PPAP form. The AIAG PPAP form also has a field asking if polymetric parts have been identified with an ISO marking code. This refers to marking plastic parts with the appropriate ISO identification for plastic parts.

There are five PPAP submission levels. The first level only requires the submission of the warrant while the second level requires the warrant with samples of the product and limited supporting data. The third level is like the second level, but with full supporting data. The final level includes the requirements of the previous level but is reviewed at the supplier's location.

DAIMLERCHRYSLER   Ford   GM   **Part Submission Warrant**

Part Name _____   Cuts. Part Number _____

Shown on Drawing No. _____   Org. Part Number _____

Engineering Change Level _____   Dated _____

Additional Engineering Changes _____   Dated _____

Safety and/or Government Regulation ☐Yes ☐ No   Purchase Oder No. _____   Weight (kg) _____

Checking Aid No. _____ Checking Aid Engineering Change Level _____   Dated _____

ORGANIZATION MANUFACTURING INFORMATION   CUSTOMER SUBMITTAL INFORMATION

Organization Name & Supplier/Vendor Code   Customer Name/Division

Street Address   Buyer/Buyer Code

City   Region   Postal Code   Country   Application

MATERIALS REPORTING
Has customer-related Substances of Concern information been reported?   ☐ Yes ☐ No ☐ n/a

Submited IMDS or other customer format: _____

Are polymetric parts identified with appropriate ISO marking codes?   ☐Yes ☐No ☐ n/a

REASON FOR SUBMISSION (Check at least one)
☐ Initial Submission   ☐ Change to Optinal Construction or Material
☐ Engineering Chang(s)   ☐ Supplier or Material Source Change
☐ Tooling: Transfer, Replacement, Refurbishment, or Additional   ☐ Change in Part Processing
☐ Correction of Discrepancy   ☐ Parts produced at Additional Location
☐ Tooling Inactive > than 1 year   ☐ Other – please specify below

REQUESTED SUBMISSION LEVEL (Ceck one)
☐ Level 1 – Warrant only (and for designated appearance items, an Appearance Approval report) submitted to customer.
☐ Level 2 – Warrant with product samles and limited supporting data submitted to customer.
☐ Level 3 – Warrant with product samles and complete supporting data submitted to customer.
☐ Level 4 – Warrant and other requirements as defined by customer.
☐ Level 5 – Warrant with product samples and complete supporting data reviewed at organization's manufacturing location.

SUBMISSION RESULTS
The results for ☐ dimensional measurments ☐ material and functional tests ☐ appearance criteria ☐ statistical process package
These results meet all design record requiorments: ☐Yes ☐ NO (If "NO" – Explanation Required)
Mold / Cavity / Production Process _____

DECLARATION
I affirm that the samples represented by this warrant are representative of out parts which were made by a process that meets all production Part Approvale Process manual 4th Edition requirements. I further affirm that these samples were produced at the production rate of ___ / ___ hours.
I also certify that documented evidence of such compliance is on file and available for review. I have noted any deviations from this declaration below.
EXPLANATION/COMMENTS: _____

Is each Customer Tool properly tagged and numbered?   ☐ Yes ☐ No ☐ n/a

Organization Authorized Signiture _____ Date _____

Print Name _____   Phone No. _____ FAX No. _____

Title _____   E-mail _____

| FOR CUSTOMER USE ONLY (IF APPLICABLE) |
PPAP Warrant Dispostion: ☐Approved ☐ Rejected ☐ Other

Customer Signature _____ Date _____

Print Name _____   Customer Tracking Number (optional) _____

March 2006   CFG-1001

Figure 5.6   Part submission warrant. (From Chrysler et al., *Production Part Approval Process (PPAP)*, 4th edn., Automotive Industry Action Group, United States, 2006.)

A full PPAP packet may include a copy of the engineering drawing with all measured measurements identified. A copy of a purchase order is also needed if the customer was responsible for the design. If the part has been changed, then an engineering change notice or some other form of customer authorization must be included. A copy of the customer's engineering approval must be included if available, otherwise a deviation permit issued by the customer to authorize limited production before PPAP approval must be included.

A flowchart is needed to show the supplier's production process for the part as well as a copy of the DFMEA and PFMEA. Although the FMEAS should be included in the PPAP, some companies consider the information in them to be proprietary because they contain the company's knowhow. In such cases, the customer should be informed of this; often, either submitting the FMEA header or reviewing the FMEA at the customer's location is a suitable alternative. A copy of the control plan should also be included in the PPAP packet; however, like the FMEA, there may be alternatives to submitting the entire control plan.

An MSA for measuring devices that will be used in the production of the part and gage R&R for critical measurements must also be included in the PPAP. A measurement report is also needed with both the actual measurements and a decision as to whether or not the results are OK. Figure 5.7 shows a PPAP dimensional analysis test report. The drawing is generally numbered with call outs on each measured dimension and the call out number is listed in the report under item number. The nominal value of specification is listed under dimension, and then the specification or tolerance limits are listed. The date the test is performed or measurements are taken needs to be listed as well as the quantity evaluated. The test or measurement results are then given and an OK or not OK decision is then made and listed in the report. The actual test results need to be described; simply listing "tested as OK" is not acceptable.

The engineering drawing must contain ballooned references to the measurements on the measurement report; this way the customer will know what the measurement corresponds to on the engineering drawing. Generally, results are available for six parts, and these parts may be sent to the customer with the PPAP depending upon the PPAP level. Material tests and other test are included in the form of a Design Verification Plan and Report (DVP&R). The laboratory's performing tests on the material must be accredited to perform the test in question.

An initial sample report is needed for the inspection of pre-prototype parts. An initial processes study is to be included to determine if the process

**Production Part Approval
Dimensional Test Results**

DAIMLERCHRYSLER [Ford] [GM]

ORGANIZATION:	PART NUMBER:
SUPPLIER/VENDOR CODE:	PART NAME:
INSPECTION FACILITY:	DESIGN RECORD CHANGE LEVEL:
	ENGINEERING CHANGE DOCUMENTS:

ITEM	DIMENSION / SPECIFICATION	SPECIFICATION / LIMITS	TEST DATE	QTY. TESTED	ORGANIZATION MEASUREMENT RESULTS (DATA)	OK	NOT OK

Blanket statements of conformance are unacceptable for any test results.

| | SIGNITURE | TITTLE | DATE |

March
2006   CFG-1003

Figure 5.7   Dimensional test results. (From Chrysler et al., *Production Part Approval Process (PPAP)*, 4th edn., Automotive Industry Action Group, United States, 2006.)

is capable. The PPAP packet must include copies of the accreditation for all laboratories that performed testing on the parts or material. If appearance is an issue, a copy of an appearance approval report must be signed by the customer and included. A master sample needs to be signed off by the customer and supplier; this sample is then maintained by either the customer or the supplier. Information must also be included on checking aids such as gages specially made for the product; a photo of the age and proof of calibration should be included. Any other customer specific requirements must also be included in the PPAP packet.

Companies supplying parts to German automobile manufacturers or their suppliers may need to use an Initial Sample Inspection Report (ISIR) in place of the previously described PPAP warrant. The ISIR form is slightly different than that of a PPAP warrant; however, the two concepts are close to each other, but may vary in the details.

5.4 Advanced Product Quality Planning

Advanced product quality planning (APQP) was developed by Ford, Chrysler, and General Motors to provide their suppliers with a common development process. Although originating in the automotive industry, the APQP concept can be applied in other industries as a quality planning tool to ensure that the customer's deadlines and quality expectations are met. Properly implemented APQP "enhances suppliers' ability to develop and produce parts and systems that satisfy their customers" (Stamatis 2001).

The use of APQP helps to reduce and manage the complexity of quality planning and can help to keep projects on schedule by the early identification of changes. It can also be helpful for communicating quality planning issues between customers and their suppliers by creating a quality plan (Chrysler et al. 2008a). There are five phases in APQP with specific actions to take during each phase. The phases are depicted in Figure 5.8.

Phase one is planning and defining the program. Once the concept has been approved the voice of the customer must be assessed; the customer's needs and specifications must be clearly understood. A business plan and marketing strategy should be started at this point. Relevant quality history data should also be analyzed. This is the phase where the concept must be approved.

The second phase is product design and development. The DFMEA should be started and engineering drawings and a preliminary bill of material should be created. Material specifications need to be defined and design reviews should be held to assess the design concept. The first prototypes should be planned and the required new gages, test equipment, machinery, and tooling must be planned. The facility layout plan for the production process needs to be started during this phase. The program should be approved

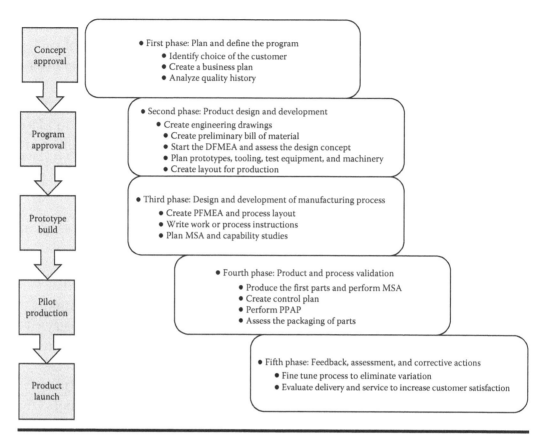

Figure 5.8   APQP phases.

at during this phase. The first prototypes should be started near the end of this phase.

Phase three is the design and development of the manufacturing process. Here, the process flowchart and floor plan need to be created. A PFMEA should be started and the required work or process instructions must be written. The needed MSA and process capability studies are also planned during this phase.

During the fourth phase both the product and process are validated. This means the first trial production runs are started, and the MSA and process capability studies are carried out. The PPAP takes place here as well as the creation of the control plan. The packaging of the parts is also assessed. The product is launched at the end of this phase. Phase five is feedback, assessment, and corrective actions. The process is fine-tuned to eliminate variation and improve customer satisfaction. The delivery and service is evaluated and improved to increase customer satisfaction.

Chapter 6

Measurement System Analysis

Measurement system analysis (MSA) is used to statistically evaluate a measurement system. An MSA assesses the accuracy of measurements; this is the difference between observed measurement results and the true value as well as the stability, which is the difference between measurements taken with the same measuring device at different times. Accuracy is sometimes also referred to as bias. It also assesses the resolution and linearity of measuring devices. Resolution is the capability to detect the smallest acceptable changes and linearity is the difference in accuracy throughout different areas in a measuring devices operating range. Precision is also assessed; this is the closeness of values when a measurement is repeated (Chrysler et al. 2010).

If a metal block has a width of 30.400 mm and a measuring device gives a result of 30.395 and a second measuring device gives a result of 30.391, then the first device is more accurate as it is closer to the true value. If the second measuring device does not give the same result a week later, but the first does, then the first measuring device has more stability. If a measuring device is not capable of measuring in millimeters and a part must be measured in millimeters, then that device does not have sufficient resolution. If a micrometer gives accurate results at the lower end of its range, but less accurate results at the higher end of its range, then it has a linearity problem.

Accuracy can be assessed by comparing the average of repeated measurements of a known reference value of a master sample. The accuracy is equal to the average of the measurements minus the reference value. The percentage of accuracy is determined by dividing the accuracy by six times the standard deviation of the measurement results.

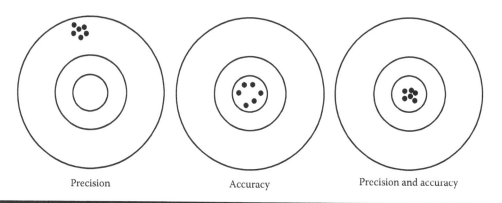

Precision   Accuracy   Precision and accuracy

Figure 6.1   Precision and accuracy.

Robin Hood hitting a target with an arrow and then splitting that arrow with a second one is an example of precision and accuracy. Good and Hardin (2012) tell of a Robin Hood parody in which Robin Hood displayed great precision by splitting two arrows; unfortunately, the arrows missed the target and were all in a nearby cow. The unfortunate cow is a great example of precision without accuracy. Figure 6.1 shows the difference between precision and accuracy.

Problems with accuracy or precision could result in a process that produces defective parts because the measuring device used for machine setup was incorrect. It is also possible that a quality problem is not actually due to a measurement out of specification, but due to a measuring device incorrectly indicating that in specification material is out of specification. The accuracy and precision of measuring devices and their operators can be assessed by performing a gage repeatability and reproducibility (R&R).

6.1 Gage Repeatability and Reproducibility

MSA uses gage R&R studies to determine if a measurement system is suitable for its intended purpose. Repeatability is the variation in repeated measurements using one measuring device with the same appraiser and the same part. Reproducibility is the average of measurements by multiple appraisers using the same measuring devices and same part.

A data collection sheet such as the one shown in Figure 6.2 is needed for collecting the data to be studied in a gage R&R. There operators measure 10 parts 3 times each. The data is then entered into the sheet, and the formulas at the bottom of the sheet can be used to create a control chart for the range. This provides a quick indication of the variability in the measuring system.

Gage Repeatability and Reproducability Data Collection Sheet											
Appraiser /Trial #	1	2	3	4	5	6	7	8	9	10	AVERAGE
A 1											
2											
3											
Average											$\bar{X}_a =$
Range											$\bar{R}_a =$
B 1											
2											
3											
Average											$\bar{X}_b =$
Range											$\bar{R}_b =$
C 1											
2											
3											
Average											$\bar{X}_c =$
Range											$\bar{R}_c =$
Part Average											$\bar{\bar{X}} =$ $R_p =$
$([\bar{R}_a = \ ] + [\bar{R}_b = \ ] + [\bar{R}_c = \ ]) / [\text{\# OF APRAISERS} = \ ] =$											$\bar{\bar{R}} =$
$\bar{X}_{DIFF} = [\text{Max } \bar{X} = \ ] - [\text{Min } \bar{X} = \ ] =$											$\bar{X}_{DIFF} =$
$*\text{UCL}_R = [\bar{\bar{R}} = \ ] \times [D_4 = \ ] =$											

$D_4 = 3.27$ for 2 trials and 2.58 for 3 trials. UCL_R represents the limit of individual R's. Circle those that are beyond this limit. Identify the cause and correct. Repeat these readings using the same appraiser and unit as originally used or discard values and re-average and recompute $\bar{\bar{R}}$ and the limiting value from the remaining observations.

Notes: _____

Figure 6.2 Gage repeatability and reproducibility data collection sheet. (From Chrysler et al., *Measurements System Analysis*, 4th edn., Automotive Industry Action Group, United States, 2010.)

Gage Repeatability and Reproducibility Report

Part No. & Name: Characteristic: Specifications:	Gage Name: Gage No: Gage Type:	Date: Performed by:

$$\bar{\bar{R}} = \qquad \bar{X}_{DIFF} = \qquad R_p =$$

Measurement Unit Analysis	% Total variation (TV)

Repeatability – Equipment Variation (EV)

$EV = \bar{\bar{R}} \times K_1$

= _____ × _____

= _____

Trials	K_1
2	0.8862
3	0.5908

$\%EV = 100\,[EV/TV]$

$= 100\,[\underline{\quad}/\underline{\quad}]$

$= \underline{\quad}\%$

Reproducibility – Appraiser Variation (AV)

$AV = \sqrt{(\bar{X}_{DIFF} \times K_2)^2 - (EV^2/(nr))}$

$= \sqrt{(\underline{\ }\times\underline{\ })^2 - (\underline{\ }^2/(\underline{\ }\times\underline{\ }))}$

$= \underline{\quad}$

Appraisers	2	3
K_2	0.7071	0.5231

$\%AV = 100\,[AV/TV]$

$= 100\,[\underline{\quad}/\underline{\quad}]$

$= \underline{\quad}\%$

Repeatability & Reproducibility (GRR)

$= \sqrt{EV^2 + AV^2}$

$= \sqrt{(\underline{\ }^2 + \underline{\ }^2)}$

_____

Parts	K_3
2	0.7071
3	0.5231
4	0.4467
5	0.4030
6	0.3742
7	0.3534
8	0.3375
9	0.3249

$\%GRR = 100\,[GRR/TV]$

$= 100\,[\underline{\quad}/\underline{\quad}]$

$= \underline{\quad}\%$

Part Variation (PV)

$PV = R_p \quad K_3$

= _____ × _____

= _____

$\%PV = 100\,[PV/TV]$

$= 100\,[\underline{\quad}/\underline{\quad}]$

$= \underline{\quad}\%$

$= \sqrt{GRR^2 + PV^2}$

$= \sqrt{(\underline{\ } + \underline{\ })}$

= _____

$= 1.41\,(PV/GRR)$

$= 1.41\,(\underline{\quad}/\underline{\quad})$

$= \underline{\quad}$

For information on the theory and constraints used in the form see *MSA Reference Manual*, 3rd edn.

Figure 6.3 Gage repeatability and reproducibility report. (From Chrysler et al., *Measurements System Analysis*, 4th edn., Automotive Industry Action Group, United States, 2010.)

The results from the data collection sheet in the Figure 6.2 can be transferred to the gage R&R report shown in Figure 6.3. The document can then be used to perform the necessary calculations and can then be saved as a report. An organization may also create their own customized version based on their need; however, the formulas should be unchanged.

The Automotive Industry Action Group guideline for MSA considers error of over 30% to be unacceptable and less than 10% is acceptable. Anything in between should be considered on a basis of importance and cost of corrections. However, the AIAG also recommends that companies decide if these guidelines fit their needs (2010), an error of 10% may be unacceptable for some measurements.

6.2 Calibration

Measuring devices may lose the ability to accurately and constantly measure over time. Surface areas may wear or the spindle on a micrometer may shift positions over time and no longer start or stop at the zero position. Measuring devices must be calibrated at regular intervals to ensure they are still functioning properly.

Measuring devices should have a calibration traceable to a national standard in an unbroken chain (see Figure 6.4). The national standard will be traceable to a reference standard. Suppose a company uses its own gage blocks to calibrate the calipers in production; there must be some way of connecting the calipers to the gage blocks that were used for the calibration. The calibrated calipers would receive a sticker; this sticker is used to identify the date the next calibration is due. The calipers are in a calibration list that contains the linkage between calibrated measuring devices and the instrument, in this case gage blocks, used to calibrate them. The gage blocks would have a calibration on file from the metrology laboratory that calibrated them,

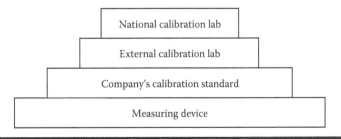

Figure 6.4   Calibration chain.

and the metrology laboratory's calibration devices would be traceable to a national standards organization such as the National Institute for Standards and Technology (NIST). The documents containing the certifications would also list the measurement uncertainty of each calibration device used.

The same concept applies to other types of measuring devices. Every measuring device will have some degree of uncertainty; the level of uncertainty must be below the level of accuracy that is needed. For an extreme example, a carpenter building a shelf using measurements in meters may need a device accurate in millimeters, but accuracy in nanometers would be both unneeded and financially wasteful.

Using un-calibrated measuring devices risks getting bad data and not knowing it. This could easily result in producing parts that a machine operator believes are in specification, when in fact all parts are out of specification because the measuring device used to set up the machine was out of calibration. If a measuring device is found to be out of calibration, checks should be performed to ensure that it was not passing defective parts or machines set up with it were properly set up.

A list of calibrated devices must be maintained. Calibration information can be stored in a CAQ program, a standalone-calibration program or in a simple spreadsheet such as the one in Figure 6.5. An organization with many measuring devices to calibrate should consider an actual calibration program over a spreadsheet. The spreadsheet may be sufficient for a smaller organization with fewer measuring devices to calibrate.

There are key pieces of information that must be in the calibration list. There should be a description of the measuring device and the serial

Calibration List										
Created by:	Modified by:	Creation Date:	Version Date:							
Serial Number	Item Type	Owner and Location	Calibration Duration	Calibration Due Date	Last Calibration Date	Calibrated By	As Found	As Left	Calibrated With	Certificate Number

Figure 6.5 Calibration list.

number of the device as well as the location and owner of the device. The duration of the calibration and the last calibration date should be listed. It is also helpful to list the due date of the next calibration. Calibration programs often provide a reminder before a calibration expires. Ideally, a spreadsheet should be programmed to change the color of the due date to yellow just prior to calibration time and red if a calibration is past due. The name of the person performing the calibration should be listed as well as the condition the measuring device was found in and the condition of the measuring device after calibration. The standard used for the calibration also needs to be listed. The calibration certificate number must be recorded if an external laboratory performed the calibration. External calibration certificates should be filed.

Chapter 7

Statistics for Quality Control

Statistical methods are often used in the field of quality. Two typical applications of statistical methods are statistical process control (SPC) and process performance and capability studies. Statistical process control monitors the performance of a process over time. Capability studies are used to get an indication as to what level of performance a process is capable of. The two methods are not mutually exclusive; capability studies can be performed as a process is created to determine the expected level of performance. If the level of performance is not acceptable, improvements should be implemented. The process can then be monitored using SPC.

The type of data used for SPC and capabilities studies matters. There are two types of data: qualitative and quantitative (see Figure 7.1). Quantitative data can be discrete to continuous. Continuous data can be measured on a continuous scale, and there is no limit to the potential values. Discrete data are count data such as the number of parts that has been rejected or rank orders such as first and second place. Qualitative data is attribute data, and it consists of labels such as boy, not OK, or green. Attribute data can be used as discrete data when the number of items in a category is counted. For example, a scratch is attribute data, but seven scratches are discrete data.

7.1 Statistical Process Control

Statistical process control (SPC) uses statistical methods to monitor a process; this results in an early warning if a problem starts to occur. A reliance on detection is a toleration of waste; prevention is a way to avoid waste

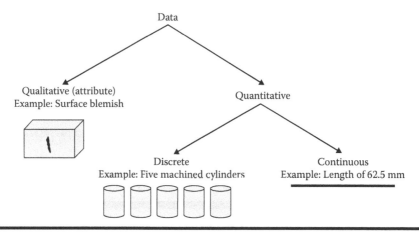

Figure 7.1 Types of data.

(DaimlerChrysler Corporation et al. 2005). The warning provided by SPC can be used to take immediate actions to correct the problem, and SPC is capable of telling the difference between random variation and actual changes in a process. The concept of SPC was developed by Dr. Walter Shewhart at Bell Labs in the 1920s and is now common in industry.

It is normal for manufactured parts to vary, although ideally the amount of variation should be very low. For example, a shaft machined to 18.5 mm might routinely vary between 18.480 and 18.520 mm. This might not be a problem if the part has a tolerance of ±1.0 mm. This variation that is normal in the process is called common cause variation. It would be a mistake to adjust a process because of common cause variation; this could result in negatively influencing a process that is functioning as well as it can. Such adjustments are called tampering. Special cause variation is an indication of changes in a process and is identified by SPC (Deming 1989). These are the changes that require corrective actions. For example, SPC can detect when a part is starting to drift out of tolerance because of tool wear. One of the advantages of SPC is the ability to detect a problem before it has occurred; the changes due to tool wear can show up in the SPC data before that part is out of specification. The need to 100% check parts to ensure quality can also be avoided by the use of SPC.

The SPC run chart shown in Figure 7.2 displays the process mean, the upper and lower control limits as well as 15 plotted data points; the final data has crossed the LCL and needs investigating. The control limits are independent of the specification, and 99.72% of all data points will be between the control limits.

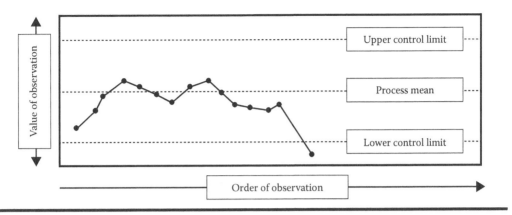

Figure 7.2 SPC chart.

The interpretation of SPC charts can be aided by using rules that provide guidance in interpreting control charts so that potential problems can be quickly detected before they occur. These rules include the Nelson (1984) rules or the Western Electric rules, which can be seen in Table 7.1. A graphic depiction of additional rules is shown in Figure 7.3.

Different types of SPC charts are used, depending upon the type of data that is being analyzed. Most types of SPC charts use rational subgroups. Rational subgroups are selected so that only common cause variation present and changes in the process can be detected (Kubiak and Benbow 2009). If a subgroup is rational, "Potential special causes of extraneous variability such as differing raw materials, personnel, spindles, test conditions and so

Table 7.1 Western Electric Rules Based on Page 6.3.2 of *NIST/SEMATECH e-Handbook of Statistical Methods*, http://www.itl.nist.gov/div898/handbook/, Version April 2012

Any point able +3 sigma limit
2 Out of the last 3 points above +2 sigma limit
4 Out of the last 5 points above the +1 sigma limit
8 Consecutive points above the center line
8 Consecutive points below the center line
4 Out of the last 5 points below the –1 sigma limit
2 Out of the last 3 points below the –2 sigma limit
Any point below the –3 sigma limit
Trend rules: 6 in a row trending up or down or 14 in a row alternating up and down

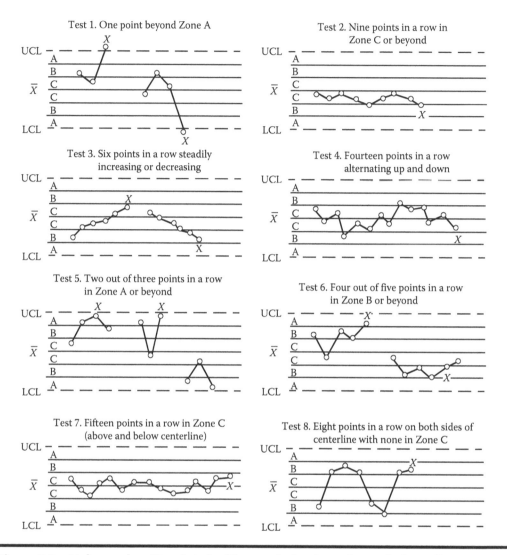

Figure 7.3 Nelson rules. (Reprinted with permission from *Journal of Quality Technology* © 1984 ASQ, www.asq.org)

on will then occur between subgroups rather than within them" (Nelson 1988). For example, a subgroup should not be collected across multiple machines or shifts. The data in the subgroup should also be independent of each other. This means that the value of one data point should have no relationship with the next data point.

Variable data, which is measured on a contentious scale, uses an individual and moving range (*ImR*) chart when the subgroup size is one. The *ImR* chart is often used when few parts are produced or it is too costly to test larger subgroups such as when an expensive product must be destroyed during testing. Subgroups greater than one can use an average and range ($\bar{X}$ and R) chart or average and standard deviation ($\bar{X}$ and S) chart. Figure 7.4 shows an $\bar{X}$ and R chart with six subgroups.

Attribute data such as the number of defects uses a c chart and the subgroup size stays constant. The subgroup is the number of items analyzed. A u chart is used for the number of defects per unit and the subgroup size can vary. Other attribute data SPC charts are the np chart for the number of defective units data with constant subgroups greater than 50 and the p chart for fraction of defective units data with a variable subgroup that is greater than 50. See Table 7.2 for attribute chart examples.

Figure 7.5 contains a flowchart for selecting the appropriate type of control chart.

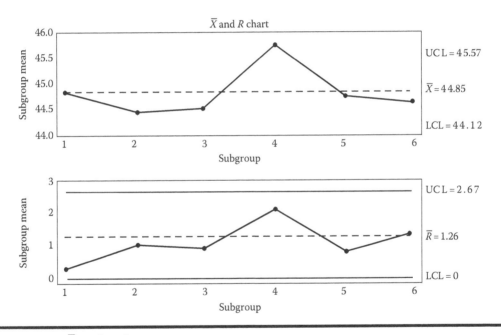

Figure 7.4 $\bar{X}$ and R chart.

Table 7.2   Attribute Chart Examples

Chart Type	Subgroup	Examples
np chart	Defectives, size is constant	Failed parts, damaged units, documents with an error
p chart	Defectives, size varies	
c chart	Defects, size is constant	Failures on a part, scratches on sheet metal, errors on a document
u chart	Defects, size varies	

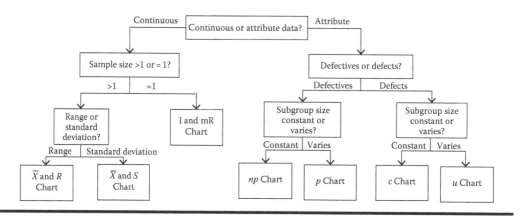

Figure 7.5   SPC flowchart.

The control limits for each type of chart are calculated by using formulas that use factors from SPC tables. There are upper control limits (UCL) and lower control limits (LCL), and they contain 99.73% of all plotted data points for a process that is in statistical control. The UCL is 3 standard deviations above the process mean and the LCL is 3 standard deviations below the process mean. The formulas for determining control limits are below in Table 7.3.

A table of factors is required for calculating control limits is available in Table 7.4.

7.2 Process Capability and Process Performance

Process capability is assessed using C_p and C_{pk}. The process performance is assessed using P_p and P_{pk} (Breyfogle 2003). The C_p and P_p calculations compare the spread of the data to the width of the tolerance limits, and C_{pk} and P_{pk} compare the process variation to the specification limits (George et al. 2005). A process can have a very good C_p or P_p but be completely out of the specification limits. The C_{pk} or P_{pk} accounts for the process mean and is calculated for both the upper and lower control limit; however, only one calculation is needed if a process only has an upper or lower control limit.

Short term data uses C_p and C_{pk} and the calculation uses the pooled standard deviation. Rational subgroups should be used for C_p and C_{pk} calculations to minimize the differences in the data within a subgroup. Long term data uses P_p and P_{pk} and the calculations use the total standard deviation. The C_p and C_{pk} indicate what the process is capable of doing. The P_p and P_{pk} indicate what the process is actually doing. The formulas for process capability and performance calculations are provided in Table 7.5.

Table 7.3 SPC Formulas

Type of Data	Description of Data	Subgroup Size	Chart Type	Center Line	Upper Control Limit	Lower Control Limit
Attribute	Number of defects	Constant size	c Chart	$\bar{c}$	$\bar{c} + 3\sqrt{\bar{c}}$	$\bar{c} - 3\sqrt{\bar{c}}$
Attribute	Number of defects per unit	Size can vary	u Chart	$\bar{u}$	$\bar{u} + 3\sqrt{\dfrac{\bar{u}}{n}}$	$\bar{u} - 3\sqrt{\dfrac{\bar{u}}{n}}$
Attribute	Number of defective units	Constant and >50	np Chart	$\overline{np}$	$\overline{np} + 3\sqrt{np(1-\bar{p})}$	$\overline{np} - 3\sqrt{np(1-\bar{p})}$
Attribute	Fraction of units defective	Can vary, is >50	p Chart	$\bar{p}$	$\bar{p} + 3\dfrac{\sqrt{\bar{p}(1-\bar{p})}}{\sqrt{n}}$	$\bar{p} - 3\dfrac{\sqrt{\bar{p}(1-\bar{p})}}{\sqrt{n}}$

(Continued)

Table 7.3 (*Continued*) SPC Formulas

Type of Data	Description of Data	Subgroup Size	Chart Type	Center Line	Upper Control Limit	Lower Control Limit
Variable	Continuous values	1	$\bar{X}$ and mR	$\bar{X} = \dfrac{\sum X_i}{n}$ and $mR = \dfrac{\sum mR_i}{n-1}$ with $\lvert X_i - X_{i-1}\rvert$ where i equals each additional value	$\bar{X} + 2.660(m\bar{R})$ and $mR = \bar{X} + 3.267(m\bar{R})$	$\bar{X} - 2.660(m\bar{R})$ and $mR = \bar{X} - 3.267(m\bar{R})$
Variable	Continuous values	>1	$\bar{X}$ and S	$\bar{\bar{X}} = \dfrac{\sum \bar{X}}{k}$ and $\bar{S} = \dfrac{\sum S}{k}$	$\bar{X} = \bar{\bar{X}} + A_3\bar{S}$ and $\bar{S} = B_4\bar{S}$	$\bar{X} = \bar{\bar{X}} - A_3\bar{S}$ and $\bar{S} = B_3\bar{S}$
Variable	Continuous values	<10 (often 5)	$\bar{X}$ and R	$\bar{\bar{X}} = \dfrac{\sum \bar{X}}{k}$ and $\bar{R} = \dfrac{\sum R}{k}$	$\bar{X} = \bar{\bar{X}} + A_2\bar{R}$ and $\bar{R} = D_4\bar{R}$	$\bar{X} = \bar{\bar{X}} - A_2\bar{R}$ and $\bar{R} = D_3\bar{R}$

Abbreviations: c, number of defects; u, number of defects per unit; np, number of defective units; p, percent defective; $\bar{X}$, process average; mR, moving range; R, range; S, process standard deviation; k, number of subgroups; n, number of observations.

Table 7.4   SPC Constants

Subgroup Size n	A_2	D_2	D_3	D_4	A_3	C_4	B_3	B_4	E_2	A_2 for Median Charts
2	1.880	1.128	0	3.267	2.659	0.798	0	3.267	2.660	1.880
3	1.023	1.693	0	2.574	1.954	0.886	0	2.586	1.772	1.187
4	0.729	2.059	0	2.282	1.628	0.921	0	2.266	1.457	0.796
5	0.577	2.326	0	2.114	1.427	0.940	0	2.089	1.290	0.691
6	0.483	2.534	0	2.004	1.287	0.952	0.030	1.970	1.184	0.548
7	0.419	2.704	0.076	1.924	1.182	0.959	0.118	1.882	1.109	0.508
8	0.373	2.847	0.136	1.864	1.099	0.965	0.185	1.815	1.054	0.433
9	0.337	2.970	0.184	1.816	1.932	0.969	0.239	1.761	1.010	0.412
10	0.308	3.078	0.223	1.777	0.975	0.973	0.284	1.716	0.975	0.362

Source: Reprinted with permission from *The Certified Quality Engineer Handbook,* ASQ Quality Press © 2009, www.asq.org

Gryna describes five assumptions that must be met before a capability study can be performed. The process must be in statistical control and the data must be normally distributed. There must also be sufficient data available to minimize sampling error, and the samples should be random and representative of the population. The individual values must also be independent of each other; there should be no correlation between consecutive measurements (2001). The sample size should be at least 100 values (George et al. 2005) to have a decent confidence level. Violation of one of these assumptions could result in reaching an incorrect concussion.

An illustration of a car and garage is often used to explain C_p and C_{pk} as shown in Figure 7.6. The garage walls represent the upper and lower specification limits, and the spread of the data represents a car. A car that is wider than the width of the garage door will fit the walls of the garage, and process data that is spread wider than the specification limits will produce out of specification parts. A process with a C_p of 1.33 will have a spread of the data that is less than the specification limits; however, the same process with a C_{pk} of 1.0 will be off-center and produce out of specification parts. Ideally, a process should have both C_p and C_{pk} of 1.33.

Table 7.5   Capability and Performance Indexes

Time Frame	Formula	Standard Deviation Formula	Use
Short term	Process capability: $$C_p = \dfrac{USL - LSL}{6S_p}$$	Pooled standard deviation $$S_p = \sqrt{\dfrac{(n_1-1)s_1^2 + (n_2-1)s_2^2 + \cdots + (K_2-1)s_K^2}{n_1 + n_2 + \cdots + K_2 - K}}$$ K is the number of subgroups	Indicates what the process is capable of relative to the width of the specification limits
	Process capability index: $$C_{pk} = \dfrac{\overline{X} - LSL}{3S_p}, \dfrac{USL - \overline{X}}{3S_p}$$		Indicates the potential ratio of the distance between process mean and specification limits
Long term	Process performance: $$P_p = \dfrac{USL - LSL}{6S_T}$$	Total standard deviation $$S_T = \sqrt{\dfrac{\sum(x - \overline{x})^2}{N-1}}$$	Indicates how the process is actually performing relative to the width of the specification limits
	Process performance index: $$P_{pk} = \dfrac{\overline{X} - LSL}{3S_T}, \dfrac{USL - \overline{X}}{3S_T}$$		Indicates the ratio of the distance between process mean and specification limits

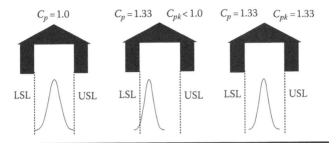

Figure 7.6   *C_p* and *C_pk* illustrated.

A process can be considered capable when the index is greater than 1.67. The process may be acceptable if the index is at least 1.33 up to 1.67. A process with an index under 1.33 should not be considered acceptable (Chrysler et al. 2006). A process with a C_p of 0.5 can be expected to produce 13.36% of parts beyond the upper or specification limit. A C_p of 1.00 would result in 0.3% of parts exceeding a specification limit and a C_p of 1.33 corresponds to 65 parts per million out of specification (ppm). A C_p of 1.63 corresponds to 1 ppm and a C_p of 2.0 can be expected to produce only parts in the upper or lower specification limit (Gryna et al. 2007).

Chapter 8

Continuous Quality Improvement

Customer's quality expectations are continuously increasing; likewise, a company's quality performance must continuously increase. To archive this, many companies implement continuous quality improvement programs. One method of achieving this continuous improvement is through the use of kaizen.

8.1 Kaizen

Kaizen is Japanese for continuous improvement. In contrast with Six Sigma projects, which seek breakthrough improvements in quality and often require significant investments in time and money, kaizen can achieve small and immediate incremental quality improvements with little costs. Kaizen improvements may be as simple as a "change in color of a welding booth from black to white to improve operator visibility" (Borrer 2009). Kaizen can be implemented by all levels of an organization, from production workers to upper management. However, the support of upper management is essential for a kaizen project to be successful.

Five whys are often used during kaizen activities to identify the true source of a problem. An example of the application of five whys for determining why a machine failed to work properly is as follows:

Why 1: Why did the machine fail to work?
         There was no control signal.
Why 2: Why was there no control signal?
         The control lever was in the wrong position.
Why 3: Why was the control lever in the wrong position?
         The control lever was worn.
Why 4: Why was it worn?
         The wear check interval was too great.
Why 5: Why was the wear check interval too great?
         The wear check interval was not in the maintenance plan.

Imai (1986) considers kaizen to be an umbrella term that encompasses a customer orientation, total quality control, an employee quality improvement suggestion system, total productive maintenance, and quality and productivity improvement.

8.2 Plan-Do-Check-Act

Kaizen uses the Plan-Do-Check-Act (PDCA) cycle, also known as the Deming Cycle or Shewhart Cycle (Imai 1986). The first step is to study the problem and form a plan for solving the problem. The second step is where the plan is implemented. After implementation, the improvement needs to be checked to ensure that it is working as planned. Modifications may be needed if it is not working according to the plan. The PDCA cycle is depicted in Figure 8.1.

One company used kaizen to determine why the cutting machines occasionally produced bad cuts. The problem was studied, and the tooling was modified once the cause of the problem was understood. Naturally, the results of the modifications were checked to compare the actual results against the expected results. Corrective actions would have been taken if there was a deviation. The corrective action was then implemented on other machines.

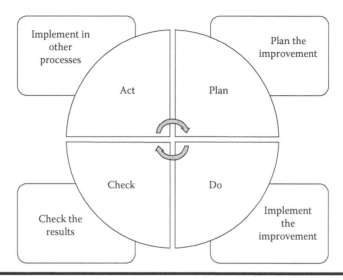

Figure 8.1 Plan-Do-Check-Act.

8.3 Root Cause Analysis

Achieving an improvement in quality often requires performing a root cause analysis (RCA). There are many reasons to perform an RCA. An RCA may be necessary due to a quality failure such as when a customer sends complaint due to a product failure or when a failure is detected within the company. It may also be necessary to perform an RCA to reduce the scrap rate for a product or to improve the delivery of a service. An RCA may be required to identify the cause of the current level of performance when a quality improvement is desired.

"There is no single RCA method for all situations; however, the RCA should involve empirical methods and the selection of the appropriate tools for the problem under investigation" (Barsalou 2015). Each situation varies and the quality tools used to reduce or eliminate failures in a machining process may not be the same as the ideal tools for increasing customer satisfaction in a service industry. There are, however, commonalities between various RCAs; quality tools should be used, a team may be necessary, and empirical evidence should always be used if possible.

The PDCA cycle can be applied to give an RCA structure with cycles for immediate actions, the investigation, and corrective actions. Immediate actions should be considered whenever a quality failure is discovered; failure to initiate immediate actions may result in defective parts reaching the customer or substandard service being performed before the root cause is found and corrective actions are implemented. Three cycles of PDCA for RCA are shown in Figure 8.2.

The first action to take upon discovering a problem is to determine how it will be addressed and what type of support may be needed so that the correct optimal team can be formed. A decision must also be made regarding a containment action. In manufacturing, this could mean inspecting parts in inventory. In a restaurant, this may mean simply cleaning a spill on the floor. The actions to take are determined by the type of problem encountered. A quality engineer encountering oily rags on the floor may remove the rags to eliminate a safety hazard and then discuss the problem with the production supervisor. A quality manager receiving a customer complaint for

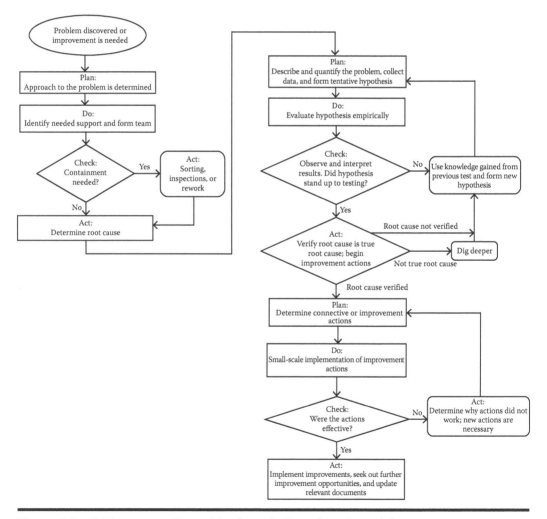

Figure 8.2   RCA process. (From Matthew A. Barsalou, Copyright 2014.)

a design problem may need the involvement of design engineers, production, logistics for blocking and controlling inventory, sales for contacting the customer, and a quality engineer for providing guidance in RCA.

The next cycle of PDCA is the actual investigation, and this phase of an investigation may need to be repeated many times, and the entire RCA process can be viewed as a helix as depicted in Figure 8.3. The first action is to describe and quantify the problem based on data. Once sufficient information is available, a tentative hypothesis can be formed using deduction. This hypothesis is then evaluated empirically. This could mean a durability test, taking measurements or performing an experiment. Ideally, even when the hypothesis was incorrect, new data will have been gained during the investigation. This information can then be used with induction to form a new hypothesis, and the cycle repeats. The root cause should be verified once it is identified. It is possible that there is either a deeper underlying root cause or the root cause may prove to be incorrect.

Quality tools such as the classic seven quality tools and the new seven management and planning tools are often helpful during an RCA. For example, an Ishikawa diagram is often very useful to support brainstorming and to list potential causes of a failure. Other situations may call for a different tool such as a run chart to view occurrences over time. The tool selected should be based upon the intended need and not simply to use the tool. Regardless of choice of tools, empiricism is still needed. Don't forget to actually look at the product that failed or the process that needs improvement.

The improvement actions should be planned once the root cause is confirmed. Whenever possible, the actions should first be tested on a small scale. It is possible that the actions will not be effective; or even worse, the actions may cause a more severe problem. Once confirmed as effective, the action or actions should be implemented. The improvements should also be implemented on other processes or products that could have the same problem. Knowledge and experience gained during the investigation should be saved as a lesson learned. Updating an FMEA or control plan is an ideal way to achieve this.

8.4 Employee Suggestion Program

An employee suggestion program is a useful tool for gathering ideas for potential Six Sigma or continuous improvement projects. Providing prompt feedback to everybody who turns in a suggestion is very important. Lack of feedback may be interpreted by employees as lack of management

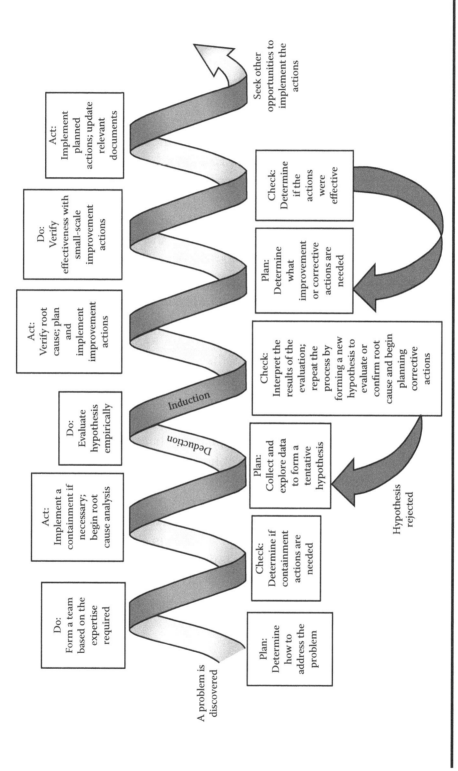

Figure 8.3 RCA helix. (From Matthew A. Barsalou, Copyright 2014.)

interest that could lead to the employee suggestion program slowly fading away. It can be helpful to provide an incentive for turning in suggestions. A cash reward based on a percentage of costs saved is one option; however, there are several disadvantages with this that should be considered. The reward may be too low to illicit interest in giving suggestions for small improvements or improvements that don't have clear financial values, such as a better way or organizing tools. Although people may like to receive cash, the intrinsic value of noncash rewards tends to be higher than the intrinsic value of cash rewards. The options for noncash rewards include merchandise with the company logo such as coffee cups and t-shirts or other small items. The value of the rewards should fit the value for the contribution with suggestions that result in major savings resulting in something more than just a coffee cup.

A simple employee suggestion program could have a locked box with suggestion forms next to it. There should be somebody responsible for checking the box at a regularly scheduled interval and all suggestions should be entered on a tracking list. The tracking list can be used for monitoring the status of the suggestion as it awaits review, and for ensuring that feedback is provided to the person who made the suggestion.

8.5 Poka-Yoke

Ideally, it should not be possible for a failure to occur. One method for aching this ideal state is poka-yoke, which is Japanese for "failure-proofing." It was originally called fool proofing; however, the name was changed to avoid implying that a worker who made a mistake is a fool (Shigeō 1987). Poka-yoke is a method of ensuring that an error can't happen such as a toaster that will not let a person lower the bread if the toaster is unplugged. The inability to depress the toast is an automatic signal that an error state exists. Another example of poka-yoke is a process where a gage is built into the production line and parts that don't fit the gage are automatically removed from the line.

Shigeō's first poka-yoke was created as a result of workers forgetting to install a spring in a simple switch. The switch was a low-cost component, but the cost of failure was high because the customer's finished product needed to be inspected every time a switch was found without a sprint. The problem was solved by the working putting two springs into a dish every time a switch was assembled. Both springs needed to be assembled into the switch and a spring left in the dish at the end of the assembly operation was a visual indicator that a spring had been forgotten (1987).

A poka-yoke may stop a process or provide some form of signal if a problem exists. Ideally, a poka-yoke device should make it impossible for a failure to occur. A common type of poka-yoke is a pin with a corresponding hole on a matching part; this is useful if the correct orientation matters, but can't be easily identified. If a mistake can't be prevented from occurring, then the poka-yoke device should ensure the defective part can't be used. Ohno gives examples of poka-yoke such as material that does not fit a tool if there is a mistake, a machine that does not start if there is a problem with the material, and a process that will not start if a process step has been forgotten (1988).

More complex poka-yoke systems can be built using a light sensor to ensure that a component is present. Another option is an automatic gaging system to ensure that a product conforms to a measurement specification such as length. For services where a physical poka-yoke is not possible, it may be helpful to use checklists to ensure tasks are completed. Ideally, the checklist should be built into the process to ensure that a failure can't happen.

8.6 Lean

Lean originated as the Toyota Production System, which in turn originated in 1956 when Taiichi Ohno of Toyota visited American automobile assembly plants. During his visit, Ohno observed the workings of American supermarkets, where customers pulled a product from the shelf when they needed it. This observation leads him to the idea that would become lean (Stroznik 2001).

Cycle-time reduction is one of the objectives of lean. This can be accomplished by eliminating nonvalue-added operations, reducing the time for value-added operations, combining several operations into one, using smaller specialized processes, moving some operations to the supplier, or back in house form the supplier and standardizing products and services (Westcott 2013). Value-added operations increase the value of a product or service. Examples include assembling multiple components into one assembly, painting a piece of sheet metal, or machining part so that it is per drawing. Nonvalue-added operations do not add value, but they may be necessary. Examples of necessary nonvalue-added process include accounting and shipping. Shipping a part to the customer does not add value to the part, but it is a necessary supporting process. Other processes may be non-value adding and unnecessary and should be eliminated.

An important lean related metrics is takt time for the rate to complete a task or process. Takt time is:

$$\text{Takt time} = \left(\frac{\text{Available time for work per period}}{\text{Demand in units per period}} \right)$$

This means there is a takt time of 12 units/hour if the demand is 96 units in an 8 hour period. An operation needing to deliver 12 units in a 160 minute period would have a takt time of 5 units/hour or 12 minutes/unit.

Just-in-time (JIT) production is often implemented as a part of lean. This means switching to a pull system where parts are only produced when there is a demand and are then delivered just-in-time. A company may use JIT for the supplier to deliver parts to the company when they are needed or one department may deliver JIT to another department. This could also mean pulling parts from storage as they are needed; however, inventory levels should be kept low to have a lean operation. Traditional manufacturing is based on a push system with parts produced independent of demand and this results in large inventories. The use of JIT is based on a pull system, with parts produced only as needed.

A signally device used to trigger the production of a part is a kanban. A kanban is often a card but can be any signaling device (Doerman and Caldwell 2010). An automatic signal can be tripped when the last part is used before more are needed or a card can be displayed where a logistic person can see it and know to deliver more parts. Kanban cards can also be used for signaling when new parts such as hardware in a storage area needs to be ordered by placing a kanban card behind the last part that can be used before more need to be ordered.

Lean also makes use of visual controls. Also known as visual factory, visual controls "are approaches and techniques that permit one to visually determine the status of a system, factory, or process at a glance and prevent or minimize process variation" (Kubiak and Benbow 2009). These visual indicators include signs, color coding of storage, and Andon boards. Andon boards are signs that signal when a process is experiencing a problem. Often, workers have the authority to stop the production line so that problems can be immediately addressed.

8.7 Seven Types of Waste

Imai tells us "Muda" is the Japanese word for waste, but this waste includes anything that does not add value (1997). This is a key concept in lean and applies equality well to both manufacturing and service industries. A manufacturing industry with waste such as the waste resulting from a high scrap rate loses money and may drive up costs. A service company with inefficient processes uses up capacity that could have been applied elsewhere and may also waste the customer's time.

According to Taiichi Ohno, there are seven types of waste: waste of overproduction, waste of time on hand (waiting), waste in transportation, waste of processing itself, waste of stock on hand (inventory), waste of movement, and waste of making defective products (1988). Eliminating waste from overproduction is one of the main points of lean. Producing more parts than needed results in costs for holding the inventory and could result in the entire inventory being inspected or scrapped if a quality problem is later discovered. Another major waste is waiting such as when a part is processed and then wastes for the next machine to be available to complete the next processing operation. There is also a waste when a machine operator needs to wait for a machine to finish a programmed operation. This time could potentially be spent in a value-added task.

Waste of movement is another common problem. Ideally, process steps should be in line so that the part does not need to be transported more than necessary. Producing defective parts is also a form of waste; detecting a defect as early as possible can prevent other defective parts from being produced and prevent the defective part from undergoing other work processes. There is no value in processing a part in added value operations for when the part has no value.

The seven wastes are sometimes renamed and reordered as "(1) transportation, (2) inventory, (3) motion, (4) waiting, (5) overproduction, (6) overprocessing, and (7) defects" and remembered using the acronym "TM WOOD" (Manos and Vincent 2012). There is also an eighth waste often added to the first seven: "unused employee potential" (Navetta 2010). Machine operators and production employees are often capable of doing far more than they are tasked with. The scope of their jobs could be expanded beyond simple tasks. For example, a production machine operator may be able to perform quality checks while waiting for a machine to finish operating. This both uses the employee's potential and reduces waiting time. Breyfogle summarizes waste as "anything other than the minimum number of people, the minimum amount of effort, material, information, and equipment necessary to add value to the product" (2008).

8.8 Five S

Whether going lean or simply implementing quality improvements, the work area should be cleaned and organized through the application of Five S before an improvement project is closed. The Five S concept is a Japanese concept for maintaining work areas. The Five S referred to in the name are based on the first letter of the Japanese words for the five steps in Five S (Imai 1997). Five S can and should be applied throughout the organization and is equally applicable in an office environment and on the production floor. The desks maybe covered in documents and production workers may need to lose time searching for tools before an organization implements Five S. Both documents and tools can be located faster after Five S implementation. An additional benefit of Five S is the positive impression it can give during a customer visit. It is doubtful that any customer was ever impressed by seeing a cluttered desk or a dirty machine. Five S can be considered "a cornerstone for companies pursuing lean" and described as "how we organize or areas to be free of clutter, efficient, safe, and pleasant to work in Manos and Vincent (2012). The exact name of the Five S steps may vary, but the actions taken are generally the same regardless of the exact name or translation from Japanese.

Step 1: Sort "Siri"
Locate unnecessary items and remove them from the work area. If a tool or document has not been needed in weeks, then maybe it should be filed or stored somewhere out of the way or be disposed of. The work area should be clutter free after this step.

Step 2: Straighten "Seiton"
Place all needed items is an easily accessible place. Tools should have a dedicated spot in a tool box or cabinet. Another simple method of tool storage is to hang the required tools from a board with the outline of the tool traced around the tool. It will quickly become clear where each tool belongs and will be obvious if a tool is missing or out of place at the end of a shift.

Step 3: Shine "Seiso"

Clean the work area and the tools and equipment in the work area.
A clean work area will be much more impressive to visitors than a filthy work area. It will also be safer than a work area with oil or grease on the floor. This step may require intensive work at the beginning of a Five S campaign. For example, years of filth may need to be removed, and the work area may need to be repainted. Once fully implemented, cleaning should turn into a simple operation to hold the gains.

Step 4: Standardize "Seiketsu"

Sorting, straightening, and shining (cleaning) should become a regularly scheduled event. One option is to perform these activities at the end of each shift. This prevents clutter from slowly building up and ensures that tools and equipment can be found by the next shift. Having a designated place for a tool will not help if the tool is not promptly returned to its storage place.

Step 5: Sustain "Shitsuke"

The previous steps must be sustained. Self-discipline will play a big role in this step. In addition to regularly scheduled cleaning a "clean as you go" mentality should be developed. For example, a screw driver should be immediately returned to its place if it is not needed anymore. Without this step, the other steps risk becoming a onetime only event with the gains lost over time.

8.9 Six Sigma

Statistical methods play a big role in Six Sigma and the DMAIC (Define, Measure, Analyze, Improve, Control) phases to provide structure to the Six Sigma project. Six Sigma is used to achieve major breakthroughs in quality and significant reductions in costs (Benbow and Kubiak 2009).

Motorola developed Six Sigma to stay competitive (Carnell 2007). The use of Six Sigma at Motorola Six Sigma led to millions in savings as well as helping Motorola to win the Malcolm Baldridge quality award. General Electric followed Motorola in the use of Six Sigma and also achieved massive savings (Breyfogle 2003). The Six Sigma methodology combines quality tools and statistical methods in a structured apache to quality improvement. Six Sigma is often called Lean Six Sigma due to the introduction of lean tools to the Six Sigma methodology. Like other approaches to quality improvement, a successful Six Sigma project requires the support of upper management to be successful.

8.9.1 DMAIC

There are five phases to a Six Sigma project using DMAIC: define, measure, analyze, improve, and control. Each phase of the first four phases contains actions that must be completed before the start of the next phase. There may be a temptation to skip a phase such as going straight to improve phase without completing the analyses phase. Such an action risks the project ending in failure and such a project should not be labeled as a Six Sigma project.

8.9.1.1 Define

Define is the first phase of a Six Sigma project. Here, the problem is clearly described and quantified. For example, "too many customer complaints for engine coils" is not a good description. A better choice would be "43 complaints for engine coils in 18 months." The problem description should be a part of a project charter; which is used like a contract between the project team and the member of management that is supporting the project. This person is the project's champion. The champion provides support at a management level such as in procuring resources and assisting if the team is being blocked.

A project statement is also created in the charter; this statement contains the project's goal and is quantified such as "reduce complaints for engine coils by 85%." A Six Sigma project also needs a scope. The scope defines the limits of the project; without a scope, there is a risk that the team will be sidetracked by issues that come up over the course of the project. The scope keeps the team on track; any new issues that arise should be dealt with after completion of the project or handed over to others outside of the project team.

The Six Sigma team is the key to a successful project; without a team, Six Sigma is merely a collection of powerful quality tools. The tools need a team to wield them, and the team is led wither by a Six Sigma Black Belt or Green Belt, depending upon the level of complexity of the project.

The team must establish a CTx (Critical to x) before the charter is ready to be approved by management. A CTx is the factor that is critical to quality in the eyes of the customer. Although the objective of a Six Sigma project may be to achieve financial savings, the project must also be looked at from the view of the customer. This is called the voice of the customer (VoC). In the engine coil example, the CTx could be the engine coil that keeps failing. The customer's main interest would not be the $90,000 that the team save their employer; it would be the improved quality that leads to lest complaints needing to be issued.

8.9.1.2 Measure

The measure phase is where the problem is evaluated in detail to establish the baseline performance. Processes are mapped using flowcharts to better understand them and capability studies are performed to see exactly how the process is behaving. Histograms and Pareto charts may also be used to understand the problem better. For example, there may be four components that fail in the engine coil; however, a Pareto chart could indicate that the majority of complaints are only for one of them. Ishikawa diagrams may also be helpful in guiding the team through brainstorming possible causes of the problem. A review of FMEAs may also yield useful information.

This is the project phase where an MSA is performed on all measuring devices that will be used during the project. Much time could be wasted if parts are measured and experiments are performed before it is discovered that the resulting variation was due to measuring devices and not the actual process.

Process capability studies are performed to understand the voice of the process. It would be difficult to attempt to improve a process before understanding what the process is capable of before improvements are made. This also provides an opportunity to improve the process once the root cause of the current level of performance is understood.

8.9.1.3 Analyze

After data has been collected and the process is understood, the analyze phase begins. Here, statistical methods are deployed to analyze data that has been previously collected. Typical statistical methods during this phase include regression, analysis of variance (ANOVA), and hypothesis testing. Naturally, other statistical methods may also be applied if needed.

Root cause analysis is also performed to identify the root cause of the problem under investigation. It is possible that statistical testing alone may point the team toward the root cause; however, statistical methods may need to be supported by other quality tools such as the classic seven. The exact tools to use should be determined based upon the problem and process under investigation.

8.9.1.4 Improve

The improve phase is where corrective actions and improvements are implemented after root causes and improvement potentials have been identified. Improvements during a Six Sigma project are not simply implemented; they are first thoroughly evaluated to ensure that they both function and have no unintended side effects. Often, design of experiments (DoE) is performed to evaluate potential improvements.

Existing FMEAs may be updated or new ones created based on the knowledge gained over the course of the project. The reevaluation or creation of FMEAs may also lead to additional improvements. The resulting FMEA actions must also be implemented.

The Six Sigma concept is transitioning into Lean Six Sigma at many companies. Regardless of whether the project is a more traditional Six Sigma project or a Lean Six Sigma project, the understanding of the process gained through the course of the project should be used to identify opportunities to make processes or operations leaner. This means shortening waiting times, reducing transportation distances, and lowering the number of pieces in inventory wherever possible.

8.9.1.5 Control

Control is the final phase of a Six Sigma project. The implemented improvements must be verified to ensure they are functioning; SPC is an ideal way to do this in the long-term. If SPC is not already in use, then it should be considered. Poka-yoke should also be implemented wherever it is possible; poka-yoke is used to prevent failures from either happening or being transferred to another step in the process.

Control plans must be updated at the end of the project; if there are no control plans, then they must be created to ensure the required checks are carried out at the designated intervals. The knowledge gained through the project must be saved so that others can benefit from this. Ideally, there should be a lessons learned database where this information can be stored. It would be wasteful if the same project needed to be started from scratch so that a different team could address a comparable project.

8.9.2 DFSS

Design for Six Sigma (DFSS) uses a Six Sigma methodology to design quality into a product or service to achieve customer satisfaction. Unlike Six Sigma, which uses DMAIC, DFSS often uses plan, identify design, optimize, and validate (PIDOV) or define, measure, analyze, design, and verify (DMADV) (Brue and Launsby 2003). Unlike the Six Sigma and DMAIC, DFSS does not have one standardized set of phases. Some companies may create their own phases to better suit their needs.

8.10 Belts and Positions in Six Sigma

There are many positions within the structure of Six Sigma. Some are highly trained and others only have an awareness of the basics of Six Sigma. A Six Sigma Black Belt has been trained and certified in the use of Six Sigma methodologies and statistical methods. Black Belts may lead Six Sigma projects themselves or may provide guidance to Six Sigma Green Belts who are leading smaller projects.

The Six Sigma Green Belt is a lower level of Six Sigma certification. Green Belts either serve as members of a Six Sigma project team or lead smaller Six Sigma projects. A Green Belt usually has fulltime responsibilities in their current position and only dedicates approximately 20% of their work time to Six Sigma projects.

Yellow and White Belts are unofficial Six Sigma positions typically awarded internally by an organization. The Yellow and White Belt typically only gets trained in a broad overview of Six Sigma and serves as a team member under the guidance of a Black Belt or Green Belt. Many companies don't even use Yellow or White Belts.

A Master Black Belt is an experienced Six Sigma Black Belt who serves as a mentor and trainer for Six Sigma Black Belts and Green Belts. Master Back Belts must be highly experienced in the application of Six Sigma and should have mastered the required statistics.

A champion is designated member of management who supports a Six Sigma project. The champion receives regular status reports and clears obstacles for the Six Sigma team. For example, the champion assists is the Six Sigma team reaches a roadblock such as resistance to change within an organization. The champion also provides needed resources to the Six Sigma team.

Chapter 9

Complaints Management

A well-functioning complaints management system is essential for managing both customer and supplier complaints. The complexity of a complaints management system can vary from company to company. A large automotive component supplier with production locations around the world may require a complex CAQ program for managing complaints. A smaller company may be able to track customer and supplier complaints in a simple spreadsheet such as the one in Figure 9.1.

A file system is needed if complaints are tracked in a spreadsheet. This could be as simple as creating a complaints folder on a server with subfolders for customer and supplier complaints. Depending on the number of customers and suppliers, additional subfolders named after the customers and suppliers may be beneficial. Additional folders should be created and named after the complaint number so that the complaint can be quickly found as shown in Figure 9.2.

An 8D report should be used for both customer and supplier complaints. The tracking list and 8D report can also be used for tracking activities related to internal quality failures. Many spreadsheet programs permit the use of hyperlinks to link documents such as an 8D report to the appropriate entry in the spreadsheet. This option can be used to link the current 8D report to the entry for the issue.

Complaint Number	Date Opened	Customer	Cust. Comp. Number	Complaint Reason	Number of Parts	Supplier	Part Number	Status	Accepted/ Rejected	Link to 8D Report	Date Closed

Figure 9.1   Complaints tracking list.

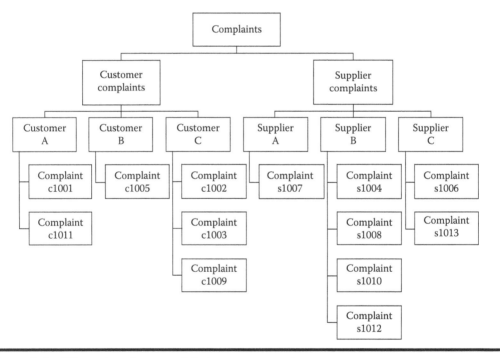

Figure 9.2   File system for complaints management.

9.1 8D Report

An 8D report is used to report on quality failures. Generally, suppliers use them to inform their customers of the status of quality complaints; however, a company can also use an 8D report for internal quality issues. Ford

Motor Company is often credited with creating the concept during the 1970s. The U.S. Military created a specification called *MIL-STD-1520C: Corrective Action and Disposition System for Nonconforming Material* (1986) in 1974 for the handling and reporting of defective supplied material; however, the specification called for a description of the nonconformance, a root cause and the disposition of the nonconforming material in a report, but this was not a true 8D report.

The name 8D refers to the eight disciplines used in the report (Rambaud 2011): D1 Team, D2 problem description, D3 containment actions, D4 root cause, D5 planned improvement actions, D6 implemented improvement actions, D7 preventative measures, and D8 congratulating the team. The top of the 8D report should contain information such as the date the complaint was opened, the last date the report was updated, the part number and the report number. It is also helpful to include 8D report number and part number of both the supplier and customer. The issue may also have a descriptive name that is listed on top of the form; for example, "missing drilled hole." The exact layout of an 8D report may vary from company to company, however, all 8D reports should contain the 8 steps even if there is a slight variation in the names used. An example of a generic 8D report can be seen in Figure 9.3.

The 8D report requires a team approach to problem solving. There must be one team leader and ideally a champion who can support the team if assistance is necessary. The team should be cross-functional; all departments involved in the issue should be represented. The problem must also be described, ideally in terms related to what the customer is claiming. The immediate action must include the person responsible for the action and the date the actions are implemented. Some complaints may require the 100% inspection of material at the customer, in transit, in the warehouse, and in production. The objective of the containment action is to protect the customer from additional failures before permanent corrective actions are implemented. This could mean that all new parts must also be checked until the root cause is understood and corrective actions are in place and confirmed to function. It may also be necessary to check other parts that could have the same problem.

Both the root cause of the occurrence and of the failure to detect the problem should be explained. A root cause investigation often requires the use of quality tools such as Ishikawa diagrams. A well detailed root cause analysis is helpful in convincing the customer that the root cause is truly understood. Planned improvement actions must be described once the

8D report Nr: Cust. 8D Nr.: Supplier 8D Nr.:	Part Nr: Cust. Part Nr.: Supplier Part Nr.:		Opened date: Version date:
Name of issue:	Customer:		Supplier:
Team leader: Team member: Team member: Team member:		Problem description:	
Containment actions:		Responsible:	Implementation date:
Root cause:			
Planned permanent corrective actions:		Responsible:	Implementation date:
Implemented permanent corrective actions:		Responsible:	Implementation date:

Actions to prevent reoccurrence:
    Work instructions_____
    Control plan_____
    DFMEA_____
    PFMEA_____
		Responsible:	Implementation date:

Congratulate the team:		Responsible:	Implementation date:

Figure 9.3   8D report.

root cause has been identified; the customer needs to be informed of the planned implementation date. The next step in an 8D report is to describe the implemented corrective actions. The ways in which these actions have been verified as effective should also be described.

The actions taken to prevent a reoccurrence of the issue need to be described. These actions include the updating of DFMEAS, PFMEAs, control plans, and work or process instructions. The objective here is to ensure that the same failure can't occur with either the same products or new, but comparable products. The 8D problem solving team must be congratulated before closing out the issue.

9.2 Customer Complaints

Companies should have a process in place for handling customer complaints promptly. According to Smith, "A company's responsiveness to complaints is crucial in maintaining a mutually beneficial business relationship" (Smith 2010). Failing to respond promptly and properly could aggravate customers and potentially risk losing either new or existing business. Having a process in place helps to mitigate the damage when a complaint does occur.

The customer should be asked for details if more information is needed. Photos of the failure and details surrounding the discovery of the failure may also be helpful. The number of failed part should also be determined. An 8D report should be sent to the customer within one day of receiving the complaint. This informs the customer that the complaint has been received and understood. It does not mean that the complaint has been accepted; acceptance or rejection of a complaint should only happen after the failure has been investigated. The initial response should describe the immediate actions that are taken. This may involve checking parts in production and in storage. It may also require checking parts at the customer or notifying the customer that an unchecked shipment is in transit. Parts inspected and found to be in specification should be labeled with "100% checked for X" if parts are sorted due to a quality issue.

A sample defect part should be requested whenever possible so that the root cause of the failure can be empirically investigated. It is possible that the failure happened due to misuse at the customer or the part may be found to be in specification. The complaints can be rejected in such situations; however, do not simply tell the customer that the complaint is rejected and close the issue. Evidence should be provided to show that the customer is at fault or that the part is in specification. Rejecting a complaint may require diplomacy and tact to be successful.

Additional actions may be needed even when the complaint is rejected. For example, a customer complaint for a part that is in specification may indicate that the specification is not correct for the customer's intended use. Failing to work with the customer to change a specification to deliver a usable product could result in the customer looking for a new supplier that can deliver a usable product.

A description of the root cause analysis should be provided in the 8D report if the complaint is accepted. This helps to reassure the customer that the cause of the problem has truly been identified. The customer should also be reassured that effective corrective actions have been identified and implemented. These actions should also be verified to ensure the effectiveness of the actions.

9.3 Supplier Complaints

Suppliers must be informed when their parts fail, even if it is a simple component. A supplier that does not know about a problem will not know that improvement actions are necessary. Such failures can reoccur and increase costs for all concerned parties.

There is also a possibility that the supplied part did not fail through any fault of the supplier. A preliminary analysis may be necessary to ensure that the failure is truly a supplier failure. The part could have been damaged in your production. It is also possible that the supplier shipped the drawing version that was ordered because the supplier did not receive the latest version of the drawing. Such situations would require internal quality improvement activities.

Like customer complaints, 8D reports can be used for supplier complaints. Here, the company is no longer writing the 8D report, but evaluating one from a supplier. The 8D report can be used as a communication tool so that the supplier can clearly explain the cause of the failure and the actions they will take to prevent a reoccurrence.

Some suppliers may refuse to issue an 8D report for a failure because "it was a simple mistake and will not happen again because we talked to the operator." Such a statement is an indication that the failure, or a comparable failure, will happen again. In such situations, supplier development may be necessary. It is crucial to communicate to the supplier the consequences of such failures. For example, increased cost due to scrap, shipping delays while waiting for replacement parts, high costs due to failure of the end product. A supplier may fail to appreciate the full impact of a two-dollar part failing after installation in a customer's expensive system.

A supplier should be provided with sufficient details to actually address the complaint. This includes providing a part number, description of the failure, and a photo of the failure, if possible. The supplier should also be offered the chance to have the part returned for detailed analysis. The supplier may need additional support in situations such as when the supplier lacks the resources for properly analyzing the failure.

The 8D report should contain the improvement actions taken as a result of a failure. These actions should be verified during the next visit to the supplier. For example, check to ensure that an FMEA was updated if the 8D report indicated that it was updated. If employees received training, check the training documents to verify that there is documentation showing the training was performed. This could mean checking all of the reported actions or just a random sample of actions from various 8D reports.

Chapter 10

Measuring Devices

Quality professionals must be knowledgeable of the physical tools of the trade: measuring devices. These are the tools that are often used to gather the information to make the correct decisions, such as comparing a product's dimension to a specification or collecting the data necessary to assess the performance of a process.

There are four types of measurement scales: nominal, ordinal, interval, and ratio (Stevens 1946). The nominal scales are based on qualitative data such as a name or label. The ordinal scales use rank order but don't indicate the degree of difference. Examples of ordinal scales include OK or not OK, good or bad. The interval scales give a degree of difference, but not a ratio between the differences. For example, 18°C is not twice as hot as 9°C. The ratio scales can be ordered to show the magnitude of the difference between values and the intervals between values are equal. For example, 18 cm is twice as long as 9 cm. Examples of scales are shown in Table 10.1.

Measuring devices should have the necessary discrimination. Generally, a discrimination of ten percent of the tolerance range is recommended. However, less discrimination may be necessary for measuring very small objects (Griffith 2003). For a tolerance range of 0.25 mm, the discrimination should be 0.025 mm. A pipe with a length tolerance range of 3 mm would need a discrimination of 0.3 mm.

Basic measuring devices include calipers, micrometers, height gages, and the surface plates required to use a height gage. Each of these types may come in different sizes and configurations. Each has an intended use, and the proper selection of measuring devices is essential for achieving precise and accurate results.

Table 10.1 Measurement Scales

Nominal Scale	Ordinal Scale	Interval Scale	Ratio Scale
OK, green, engineer	First place, heaviest, smallest	Degree celsius, calendar years	Length (cm), weight (kg), speed (mph)

One of the most basic measuring devices is the Vernier caliper. Vernier calipers have a sliding Vernier assembly with a movable measuring jaw and a stationary bar with a fixed measuring jaw (Cubberly and Kakerjian 1989). The stationary bar has a line scale and the Vernier assembly has a Vernier scale. The piece being measured is clamped in the jaws, and the line scale and Vernier scale are used to determine the measurements of the piece. The jaws are used to measure an outside distance such as the outside diameter of a tube. Many Vernier calipers also have measuring blades for inside measurements such as the inside diameter of a tube. Many calipers also have a depth bar and the end for measuring depth as shown in Figure 10.1.

To read Vernier calipers, the value for the first line on the stationary bar to line up with a line on the Vernier scale is receded. The line on the Vernier scale that lines up exactly with a line on the stationary bar is also recorded, and the two values are added together to give the measurement.

Calipers may have a dial indicator as shown in Figure 10.2 or a digital readout as shown in Figure 10.3. Some digital calipers have the capability to be connected to a data storage device so that the operator only needs to take a measurement and the results are automatically stored. This can be advantageous when using calipers to collect SPC data. There are many types of specialized calipers available such as one used for inside measurements and shown in Figure 10.4.

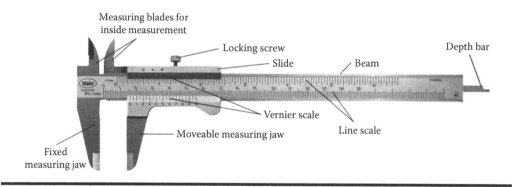

Figure 10.1 Vernier calipers. (Courtesy of Mahr Federal Inc., Providence, RI.)

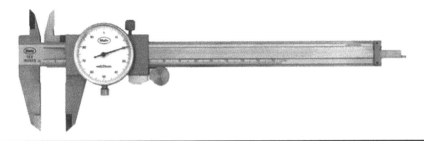

Figure 10.2 Calipers with dial indicator. (Courtesy of Mahr Federal Inc., Providence, RI.)

Figure 10.3 Digital calipers. (Courtesy of Mahr Federal Inc., Providence, RI.)

Figure 10.4 Inside digital calipers. (Courtesy of Mahr Federal Inc., Providence, RI.)

Figure 10.5 shows a micrometer with a Vernier scale. The thimble is used to close the spindle so that the measured piece is between the spindle and the anvil. The ratchet is then used to lightly tighten the spindle to get an accurate measurement. Micrometers are more exact than calipers.

Figure 10.6 shows example of a measurement from a Vernier micrometer. There are two lines visible on the top of the sleeve so the value 2.0 should be recorded. The graduations for the lower lines are 0.5 mm each so the value 0.5 should be recorded. The line on the sleeve lines up with the value 0.28 mm on the thimble so the value 0.28 should be recorded. The total value is 0.5 + 2.0 + 0.28 = 2.78.

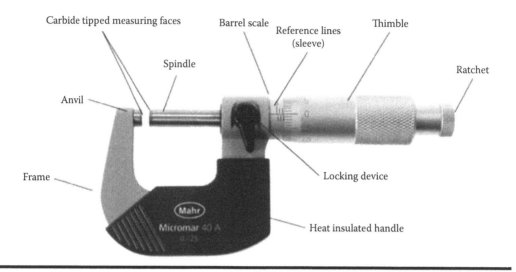

Figure 10.5   Vernier micrometer. (Courtesy of Mahr Federal Inc., Providence, RI.)

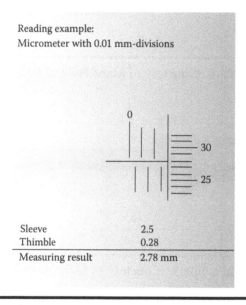

Reading example:
Micrometer with 0.01 mm-divisions

Sleeve	2.5
Thimble	0.28
Measuring result	2.78 mm

Figure 10.6   Reading a micrometer. (Courtesy of Mahr Federal Inc., Providence, RI.)

Like calipers, there are many types of micrometers available. Digital calipers are shown in Figure 10.7; like calipers, some digital micrometers can be connected to a data collection device so that data is stored when the operator pushes a button. Figure 10.8 shows calipers for measuring larger lengths, and Figure 10.9 shows a micrometer with a dial indicator in place of a Vernier scale. There are also many specialized type of calipers available (Walker 2000) such as the one shown in Figure 10.10; this micrometer is used for measuring depths.

Figure 10.7   Digital micrometer. (Courtesy of Mahr Federal Inc., Providence, RI.)

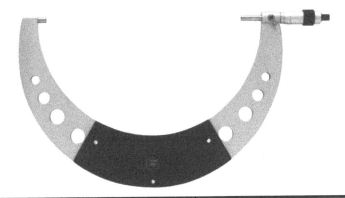

Figure 10.8   Micrometer. (Courtesy of Mahr Federal Inc., Providence, RI.)

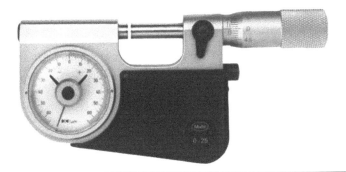

Figure 10.9   Micrometer with dial indicator. (Courtesy of Mahr Federal Inc., Providence, RI.)

Test indicators "measure displacements that occur in a direction perpendicular to the shaft of the contact point" (Rufe 2002). The test indicator can be used for taking a direct measurement or for making a comparison between a work piece and a reference piece. Using a test indicator with the stylus tip at an angle may result in a cosine error. Figure 10.11 shows a test indicator with a dial, and Figure 10.12 shows a digital test indicator. Test indicators are mounted on a stand as shown in Figure 10.13.

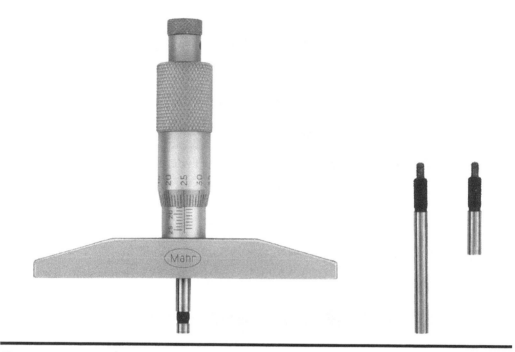

Figure 10.10   Depth micrometer. (Courtesy of Mahr Federal Inc., Providence, RI.)

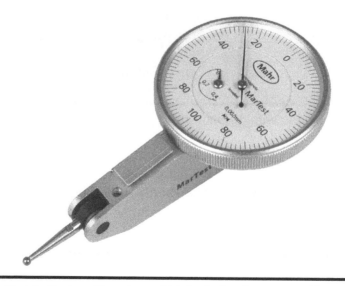

Figure 10.11   Test indicator. (Courtesy of Mahr Federal Inc., Providence, RI.)

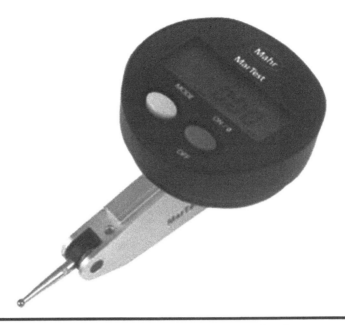

Figure 10.12 Digital test indicator. (Courtesy of Mahr Federal Inc., Providence, RI.)

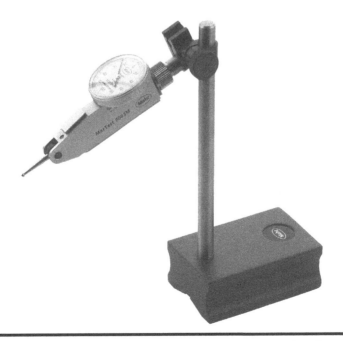

Figure 10.13 Test indicator on a dovetailed stand. (Courtesy of Mahr Federal Inc., Providence, RI.)

Another type of indicator is a dial indicator (see Figure 10.14). The dial indicator can be used for purposes such as testing the roundness of a cylindrical object such as a tube. The dial indicator is set to zero after the probe is resting on the surface of the measuring piece. To test for roundness, the work piece is rotated and the dial is observed. There are also digital versions available such as the one in Figure 10.15. The dial indicators are mounted on a stand such as the one in Figure 10.16.

There are many types of measuring gages available such as the one in Figure 10.17 for taking internal measurements and the one in Figure 10.18 for measuring depth. Figure 10.19 shows a digital bevel protector for measuring angles. Other types of dial gages include bore gages thickness gages and air gages.

Surface plates (Figure 10.20) are granite blocks with a very smooth surface that can be used as a reference surface. Surface plates come in grades, AA laboratory grade, A inspection grade, and B tool room grade (Griffith 2003). The surface plates can be used together with height gages such as the one in Figure 10.21. The height gage is placed on the surface plate and the measuring tip is zeroed against the surface plate. The measuring tip is then raised above the measuring piece, and the measuring piece is placed under the measuring tip. The measuring tip is then lowered till it touches the surface of the measuring piece, and the results are read on the height gage. The height gages can be digital, use a dial, or have Vernier scales.

Figure 10.14   Dial indicator. (Courtesy of Mahr Federal Inc., Providence, RI.)

Figure 10.15   Digital indicator. (Courtesy of Mahr Federal Inc., Providence, RI.)

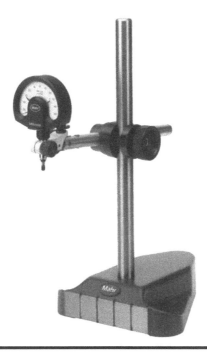

Figure 10.16   Dial indicator on an indicator stand. (Courtesy of Mahr Federal Inc., Providence, RI.)

Figure 10.17   Gage for internal measurements. (Courtesy of Mahr Federal Inc., Providence, RI.)

Figure 10.18   Indicating depth gage. (Courtesy of Mahr Federal Inc., Providence, RI.)

Often, a V block is used to hold the piece being measured. Many V blocks such as the one in Figure 10.22 has a magnet, which can be applied to the V surface by turning a knob. This helps to keep the workspace firmly in place so that it does not move while being measured. A good measurement lab or tool room will have many different combinations of V blocks available to accommodate different measuring pieces.

Gage blocks are used for both calibrating other measuring devices and for taking measurement. Gage blocks come in steel (Figure 10.23) and ceramic (Figure 10.24). They are frequently referred to as Johansson blocks, or more commonly, Jo blocks.

Figure 10.19   Digital universal bevel protractor. (Courtesy of Mahr Federal Inc., Providence, RI.)

Figure 10.20   Surface plate on a stand. (Courtesy of Mahr Federal Inc., Providence, RI.)

The federal specification for gage blocks, GGG-G-15C, lists four classes of gage blocks; Grade 0.5 for high precision gaging, Grade 1 laboratory gage blocks for calibration of inspection gage blocks and precision gaging, Grade 2 tool room and inspection standards, and grade 3 for use as shop standards (Oberg et al. 2000).

The ISO standard 3650 also lists four classes of gage blocks. Calibration class K is used for the calibration of other gage blocks. Calibration class 0 is used for the calibration of high precision instruments and tolerance class 1

Figure 10.21   Height gage. (Courtesy of Mahr Federal Inc., Providence, RI.)

Figure 10.22   V block. (Courtesy of Mahr Federal Inc., Providence, RI.)

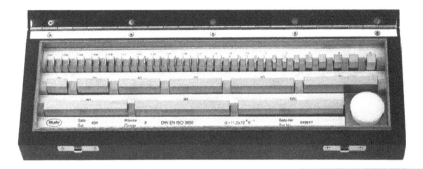

Figure 10.23   Steel gage block set. (Courtesy of Mahr Federal Inc., Providence, RI.)

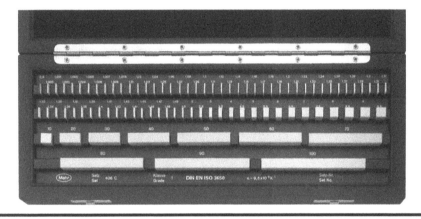

Figure 10.24   Ceramic gage block set. (Courtesy of Mahr Federal Inc., Providence, RI.)

is used for setting indicating gages and checking other gages as well as for taking measurements. Tolerance class 2 is used for checking the dimensions of jigs (Mahr 2014).

The correct gage block size is not always available, but gage blocks can be combined into the appropriate size by wringing them; the blocks are placed beside each other forming an X and then twisted into position side-by-side while pressure is applied (Oberg et al. 2000). The gage blocks then hold together and can be used for measuring purposes. Gage blocks should never be stored in a wrung position and should be replaced if they are ever rusted, damaged, or pitted. Gage blocks that no longer wring together may have additional problems that can affect accuracy and should also be replaced.

Diameters such as bored holes can be measured using pin gages. Figure 10.25 shows pin gages with and without handles and Figure 10.26 shows pin gages in a pin gage box. Pins are inserted into the diameter

Figure 10.25   Pin gages without a handle and with a handle. (Courtesy of Mahr Federal Inc., Providence, RI.)

Figure 10.26   Pin gage set. (Courtesy of Mahr Federal Inc., Providence, RI.)

that is being checked. Pins smaller than the diameter will fit loosely and pins larger than the diameter will not fit. The correct size should have a snug fit.

Gage rings (Figure 10.27) are used to check outside diameters. They can be used as go/no-go gages and for the calibration of indicators. Ring gages may come in sets for use as go/no-go gages, in such situations; the no-go ring gage will have a grove on the outside for quick identification (Griffith 2003). There are also thread gages such as the ones shown in Figures 10.28 and 10.29. One gage is used for checking the threads in a threaded hole, and the ring like gage is used for checking the threads on the matching bolt or threaded part.

Figure 10.27   Gage ring. (Courtesy of Mahr Federal Inc., Providence, RI.)

Figure 10.28   Thread setting plug gage. (Courtesy of Mahr Federal Inc., Providence, RI.)

Figure 10.29   Ring gage. (Courtesy of Mahr Federal Inc., Providence, RI.)

References

Aitken, H.J.G. 1985. *Scientific Management in Action: Taylorism at the Watertown Arsenal, 1908–1915*. Princeton, NJ: Princeton University Press.

Akao, Y. (ed.). 1990. *Quality Function Deployment: Integrating Customer Requirements into Product Design*. (Translated by Glenn H. Mazur). Portland, OR: Productivity Press.

Akao, Y. (ed.). 1991. *Hoshin Kanri: Policy Deployment for Successful TQM*. (Translated by Glenn H. Mazur). New York: Productivity Press.

Arter, D.R. 2003. *Quality Audits for Improved Performance*. 3rd edn. Milwaukee, WI: ASQ Quality Press.

Arter, D.R. and J.P. Russell. 2009. ISO Lesson Guide 2008: Pocket Guide to ISO 9001:2008. 3rd edn. Milwaukee, WI: ASQ Quality Press.

Barsalou, M.A. 2015. *Root Cause Analysis: A Step-by-Step Guide to Using the Right Tool at the Right Time*. New York: Productivity Press.

Borrer, C.M. (ed.). 2009. *The Certified Quality Engineer Handbook*. 3rd edn. Milwaukee, WI: ASQ Quality Press.

Brassard, M. 1996. *The Memory Jogger Plus: Featuring the Seven Management and Planning Tools*. Salem, NH: GOAL/QPC.

Breyfogle III, F.W. 2003. *Implementing Six Sigma: Smarter Solutions Using Statistical Methods*. 2nd edn. Hoboken, NJ: John Wiley & Sons, Inc.

Breyfogle III, F.W. 2008. *Integrated Enterprise Excellence, Volume II—Business Deployment: A Leader's Guide for Going beyond Lean Six Sigma and the Balanced Scorecard*. Austin, TX: Bridgeway Books/Citus Publishing.

Brue, G. and R.G. Launsby. 2003. *Design for Six Sigma*. New York: McGraw Hill.

Butman, J. 1997. *Juran: A Lifetime of Influence*. New York: John Wiley & Sons.

Carnell, M. 2007. Six Sigma in everything we do? *Quality Progress* 40(1): 67–68.

Chow, A. 2007. One good idea: Compliance requirement matrix. *Quality Progress* 40(12): 80.

Chrysler, Ford, and General Motors. 2006. *Production Part Approval Process (PPAP)*. 4th edn. United States: Automotive Industry Action Group.

Chrysler, Ford, and General Motors. 2008a. *Advanced Product Quality Planning and Control Plan: APQP*. 2nd edn. United States: Automotive Industry Action Group.

Chrysler, Ford, and General Motors Supplier Quality Requirements Task Force. 2008b. *Potential Failure Modes and Effects Analysis (FMEA)*. 4th edn. United States: Automotive Industry Action Group.

Chrysler, Ford, and General Motors. 2010. *Measurements System Analysis*. 4th edn. United States: Automotive Industry Action Group.

Cole, R.E. 1999. *Managing Quality Fads: How American Business Learned to Play the Quality Game*. New York: Oxford University Press.

Colletti, J. 2013. *The Hoshin Kanri Memory Jogger: Processes, Tools, and Methodology for Successful Strategic Planning*. Salem, NH: Goal/QPC.

Crosby, P.B. 1980. *Quality is Free: The Art of Making Quality Certain*. New York: Mentor.

Crosby, P.B. 1999. Quality and Me: Lessons from an evolving life. San Francisco, Jossey Bass Publishers.

Cubberly, W.H. and R. Kakerjian (ed.). 1989. *Tool and Manufacturing Engineers Handbook: Desk Edition*. Dearborn, MI: Society of Manufacturing Engineers.

Daimler Chrysler Corporation, Ford Motor Company, and General Motors Corporation. 2005. *Statistical Process Control (SPC)*. 2nd edn. United States: Automotive Industry Action Group.

De Feo, J. 2010. Strategic planning and deployment: Moving from good to Great. In: *Juran's Quality Handbook*. 6th edn. Juran, J.M. and J.A. De Feo, eds. New York: McGraw-Hill.

De Feo, J. and J.M. Juran. 2014. *Juran's Quality Essentials for Leaders*, pp. 227–254. New York: McGraw Hill.

Deming, W.E. 1989. *Out of the Crisis*. Cambridge, MA: Massachusetts Institute of Technology.

Deming, W.E. 1994. *The New Economics: For Industry, Government, Education*. 2nd edn. Cambridge, MA: The MIT Press.

Doerman, S.M. and R.K. Caldwell. 2010. Lean techniques: Improving process efficiency. In: *Juran's Quality Handbook*. 6th edn. Juran, J.M. and J.A. De Feo, eds., pp. 327–354. New York: McGraw-Hill.

Duffy, G., S.A. Laman, P. Mehta, G. Ramu, N. Scriabina, and K. Wagoner. 2012. Beyond the basics. *Quality Progress* 45(6): 18–29.

Dunmire, T. 2014. Standards outlook: Missing in action. *Quality Progress* 47(9): 52–53.

Feigenbaum, A.V. 1983. *Total Quality Control*. New York: McGraw-Hill.

Fine, D.L. and W.L. Read. 2000. A blueprint for document control. *Quality Progress* 33(3): 65–69.

George, M.L., D. Rowlands, M. Price, and J. Maxey. 2005. *The Lean Six Sigma Pocket Tool Book*. New York: McGraw-Hill.

Good, P.I. and J.W. Hardin. 2012. *Common Errors in Statistics (and How to Avoid Them)*. Hoboken, NJ: John Wiley & Sons, Inc.

Griffith, G.K. 2003. *The Quality Technician's Handbook*. 5th edn. Upper Saddle River, NJ: Prentice Hall.

Gryna, F.M. 2001. *Quality Planning and Analysis*. 4th edn. New York: McGraw-Hill.

Gryna, F.M., R.C. Chua, and J.A. De Feo. 2007. *Quality Planning and Analysis.* 5th edn. New York: McGraw-Hill.

Hannon, C. and S. Grossman. 2011. Put JIB on the Job. *Quality progress.* 44(7): 30–35.

Heizer, J. and B. Render. 2001. *Principles of Operations Management.* Upper Saddle River, NJ: Prentice Hall.

Hounshell, D.A. 1984. *From the American System to Mass Production 1800–1932: The Development of Manufacturing Technology in the United States.* Baltimore, MD: The Johns Hopkins University Press.

Imai, M. 1986. *Kaizen: The Key to Japan's Competitive Success.* New York: McGraw Hill.

Imai, M. 1997. *Gemba Kaizen: A Commonsense, Low-Cost Approach to Management.* New York: McGraw Hill.

Ishikawa, K. 1985. *What is Total Quality Control: The Japanese Way.* (Translated by D.J. Lu). Englewood Cliffs, NJ: Prentice Hall.

Ishikawa, K. 1991. *Guide to Quality Control.* 2nd edn. (Translated by Asian Productivity Organization). Tokyo, Japan: Asian Productivity Organization.

ISO 9000:2005. 2005. *Quality Management Systems—Fundamentals and Vocabulary.* Geneva, Switzerland: International Organization for Standardization.

ISO 9001:2000. 2000. *Quality management systems—Requirements.* Geneva, Switzerland: International Organization for Standardization.

ISO 9001:2008. 2008. *Quality Management Systems—Particular Requirements.* Geneva, Switzerland: International Organization for Standardization.

ISO 9004:2009. 2009. *Quality Management Systems—Guidelines for Performance Improvement.* Geneva, Switzerland: International Organization for Standardization.

ISO 13485:2003. 2003. *Medical Devices—Quality Management Systems— Requirements for Regulatory Purposes.* Geneva, Switzerland: International Organization for Standardization.

ISO/TS 16949:2009. 2009. *Quality Management Systems—Particular Requirements for the Application of ISO 9001:2008 for Automotive Production and Relevant Service Part Organizations.* Geneva, Switzerland: International Organization for Standardization.

Johnson, K. 2001. Phillip B. Crosby's mark on quality. *Quality Progress* 34(10): 25–30.

Juran, J.M. 1975. The non-pareto principle—Mea Culpa. *Quality Progress* 8(95): 8–9.

Juran, J.M. 1988. How to use the handbook. In: *Juran's Quality Control Handbook.* 4th edn. Juran, J.M. and F.M. Gryna, eds. pp. 1.1–1.5. New York: McGraw-Hill.

Juran, J.M. 1992. *Juran on Quality by Design: The New Steps for Planning Quality into Goods and Services.* New York: The Free Press.

Juran, J.M. 1995a. *Managerial Breakthrough: The Classic Book on Improving Management Performance.* (Revised edn.). New York: McGraw-Hill.

Juran, J.M. (ed.). 1995b. *A History of Managing for Quality: The Evolution, Trends, and Future Directions of Managing for Quality.* Milwaukee, WI: ASQC Quality Press.

Juran, J.M. 1997. Early SQC: A historical supplement. *Quality Progress* 30(9): 73–81.

Juran, J.M. 2004. *Architect of Quality: The Autobiography of Dr. Joseph M. Juran.* New York: McGraw Hill.

Juran, J.M. and J.A. De Feo (ed.). 2010. *Juran's Quality Handbook.* 6th edn. New York: McGraw-Hill.

Kaplan, R.S. and D.P. Norton. January–February 1992. The balanced scorecard—Measures that drive performance. *Harvard Business Review* 70(1): 71–79.

Kaplan, R.S. and D.P. Norton. 1996. *The Balanced Scorecard.* Cambridge, MA: Harvard Business Review Press.

Kemp, S. 2006. *Quality Management Demystified: A Self-Teaching Guide.* New York: McGraw Hill.

Kerzner, H. 1998. *Project Management: A Systems Approach to Planning, Scheduling, and Controlling.* 6th edn. New York: John Wiley & Sons, Inc.

Kubiak, T.M. and D.W. Benbow. 2009. *The Certified Six Sigma Black Belt Handbook.* Milwaukee, WI: ASQ Quality Press.

Laman, S.A. 2011. Back to basics: A tool for anyone. *Quality Progress* 44(5): 72.

Lazarte, M. November 5, 2014. ISO 9001 revision moves on to final stage. ISO. Retrieved November 30, 2014. http://www.iso.org/iso/home/news_index/news_archive/news.htm?refid=Ref1905.

Liebesman, S. 2013. Standards outlook: Work in progress. *Quality Progress* 46(11): 52–53.

Mahr. Catalog: Dimensional metrology. 2011. Retrieved November 17, 2014. http://www.mahr.com/images/OnlineKataloge/Mahr-Metrology-Catalog-EN-2011/blaetterkatalog/index.html.

Manos, A. and C. Vincent (ed.). 2012. *The Lean Handbook: A Guide to the Bronze Certification Body of Knowledge.* Milwaukee, WI: ASQ Quality Press.

Mitchell, G. 1998. *The Trainer's Handbook: The AMA Guide to Effective Training.* 3rd edn. New York: American Management Association.

Naden, C. May 16, 2014. ISO draft now available for public comment. ISO. Retrieved November 30, 2014. http://www.iso.org/iso/home/news_index/news_archive/news.htm?refid=Ref1850.

Navetta, J. 2010. One good idea: Number nine. *Quality Progress* 43(8): 64.

Nelson, L.S. 1984. Technical aids: The Shewhart control chart-tests for special causes. *Journal of Quality Technology* 16(4): 238–239.

Nelson, L.S. 1988. Technical aids: Control charts: Rational subgroups and effective applications. *Journal of Quality Technology* 20(1): 73–75.

NIST/SEMATECH. 2012. *e-Handbook of Statistical Methods.* http://www.itl.nist.gov/div898/handbook/. Accessed July 23, 2015.

Niven, P.R. 2014. *Balanced Scorecard Evolution: A Dynamic Approach to Strategy Execution.* Hoboken, NJ: John Wiley & Sons, Inc.

Oberg, E., F.D. Jones, H.L. Horton, and H.H. Ryffel. 2000. *Machinery's Handbook.* 26th edn. New York: Industrial Press Inc.

Ohno, T. 1988. *Toyota Production System: Beyond large-Scare Production.* (Translation by Productivity, Inc.). Portland, OR: Productivity Press.

Palmes, P. 2014. A new look: 15 things you must know about the upcoming ISO 9001 revision. *Quality Progress* 47(9): 16–21.

Parsowith, B.S. 1995. *Fundamentals of Quality Auditing.* Milwaukee, WI: ASQC Quality Press.

Phillips, A.W. 2009. *ISO 9001:2008 Internal Audits Made Easy: Tools, Techniques, and Step-by-Step Guidelines for Successful Internal Audits.* 3rd edn. Milwaukee, WI: ASQ Quality Press.

Phillips-Donaldson, D. 2004. Unsung heroes of quality. *Quality Progress* 37(11): 79–82.

Pompeo, J. (ed.). 2003. *TL 9000 Quality Management Systems Requirements Handbook.* 3rd edn. United States: American National Standards Institute.

Rambaud, L. 2011. *8D Structured Problem Solving: A Guide to Creating High Quality 8D Reports.* 2nd edn. Breckenridge, CO: PHRED Solutions.

ReVelle, J.B. 2004. *Quality Essentials: A Reference Guide from A to Z.* Milwaukee, WI: ASQ Quality Press.

Richman, L. 2011. *Improving Your Project Management Skills.* 2nd edn. New York: American Management Association.

Robinson, M. 1982. The QC circles: A practical guide. Ringwood, IK: Gower.

Rufe, P.D. 2002. *Fundamentals of Manufacturing.* 2nd edn. Dearborn, MI: Society of Manufacturing Engineers.

Russell, J.P. 2007. *The Internal Auditing Pocket Guide.* 2nd edn. Milwaukee, WI: ASQ Quality Press.

Shigeō, S. 1987. *The Sayings of Shigeo Shingo: Key Strategies for Plant Improvement.* (Translated by A.O. Dillon). Cambridge, MA: Productivity Press.

Shewhart, W.A. 1980. *Economic Control of Quality of Manufactured Product/50th Anniversary Commemorative Issue.* Milwaukee, WI: ASQ Quality Press.

Shewhart, W.A. 1986. *Statistical Method from the Viewpoint of Quality Control.* Mineola, NY: Dover Publications.

Sittsamer, M.J., M.R. Oxley, and W. O'Hara. November 2007. Turbocharge your preventative action system. *Quality Progress* 40(11): 37–42.

Smith, J.B. 2010. Back to basics: Rapid response. *Quality Progress* 43(7): 72.

Society of Automotive Engineers. 2009. *AS 9000 Quality Management Systems—Requirements for Aviation, Space and Defense Organizations.* United States: Society of Automotive Engineers.

Stamatis, D.H. 2001. *Advanced Quality Planning: A Common Sense Guide to AQP and APQP.* New York: Productivity Press.

Stevens, S.S. 1946. On the theory of scales of measurement. *Science* 7(2684): 677–680.

Stevenson, W.J. 1999. *Production/Operations Management.* 6th edn. New York: McGraw Hill.

Stroznik, P. 2001. Toyota alters face of production. *Industry Week* 250(11): 46–48.

Tague, N.R. 2005. *The Quality Toolbox.* 2nd edn. Milwaukee, WI: ASQ Quality Press.

U.S. Department of Defense. 1986. *MIL-STD-1520C: Corrective Action and Disposition System for Nonconforming Material.* Washington, DC: Department of Defense.

VDA 6.1. 2000. *Qualitätsmanagement in der Automobilindustrie: QM-System Audit* (*Quality Management in the Automotive Industry: QM-System Audit*). (Title translated by author). Frankfurt, Germany: VDA.

Walker, J.R. 2000. *Machining Fundamentals: From Basic to Advanced Techniques.* Tinley Park, IL: The Goodheart-Willcox Company, Inc.

Watson, G. 2004. The legacy of Ishikawa. *Quality Progress* 37(4): 54–57.

Watson, G. 2005. Timeless wisdom from Crosby. *Quality Progress* 38(6): 64–67.

Westcott, R.T. (ed.). 2013. *The Certified Manager of Quality/Organizational Excellence Handbook.* 4th edn. Milwaukee, WI: ASQ Quality Press.

Wrestler, D. 2014. Career corner: The Pizza paradigm. *Quality Progress* 47(11): 50–51.

Glossary*

Accreditation: Certification by a recognized body of the facilities, capability, objectivity, competence, and integrity of an agency, service or operational group or individual to provide the specific service or operation needed. The term has multiple meanings depending on the sector. Laboratory accreditation assesses the capability of a laboratory to conduct testing, generally using standard test methods. Accreditation for health-care organizations involves an authoritative body surveying and verifying compliance with recognized criteria, similar to certification in other sectors.

Accreditation body: An organization with authority to accredit other organizations to perform services such as quality system certification.

Accuracy: The characteristic of a measure.

Activity network diagram: An arrow diagram used in planning.

Advanced Product Quality Planning (APQP): High-level automotive process for product realization, from design through production part approval.

Affinity diagram: A management tool for organizing information (usually gathered during a brainstorming activity).

Alignment: Actions to ensure that a process or activity supports the organization's strategy, goals, and objectives.

American National Standards Institute (ANSI): A private, nonprofit organization that administers and coordinates the U.S. voluntary standardization and conformity assessment system. It is the U.S. member body in the International Organization for Standardization, known as ISO.

---

* Reprinted with permission from *Quality Progress* © 2015, www.asq.org

American National Standards Institute–American Society for Quality (ANSI–ASQ): An organization that accredits certification bodies for ISO 9001 quality management systems, ISO 14001 environmental management systems, and other industry specific requirements.

Andon board: A production area visual control device, such as a lighted overhead display. It communicates the status of the production system and alerts team members to emerging problems (from Andon, a Japanese word meaning "light").

Appraisal cost: The cost of ensuring an organization is continually striving to conform to customers' quality requirements.

Arrow diagram: A planning tool to diagram a sequence of events or activities (nodes) and their interconnectivity. It is used for scheduling and especially for determining the critical path through nodes.

AS9100: An international quality management standard for the aerospace industry published by the Society of Automotive Engineers and other organizations worldwide. It is known as EN9100 in Europe and JISQ 9100 in Japan. The standard is controlled by the International Aerospace Quality Group (see listing).

Asia Pacific Laboratory Accreditation Cooperation (APLAC): A cooperative of laboratory accreditation bodies.

Assessment: A systematic evaluation process of collecting and analyzing data to determine the current, historical, or projected compliance of an organization to a standard.

Assignable cause: A name for the source of variation in a process that is not due to chance and, therefore, can be identified and eliminated. Also called "special cause."

Association for Quality and Participation (AQP): Was an independent organization until 2004, when it became an affiliate organization of ASQ. Continues today as ASQ's Team and Workplace Excellence Forum.

Attribute data: Go/no-go information. The control charts based on attribute data include percent chart, number of affected units chart, count chart, count per unit chart, quality score chart, and demerit chart.

Attributes, method of: The method of measuring quality that consists of noting the presence (or absence) of some characteristic (attribute) in each of the units under consideration and counting how many units do (or do not) possess it. Example: go/no-go gauging of a dimension.

Audit: The on-site verification activity, such as inspection or examination, of a process or quality system, to ensure compliance to requirements.

An audit can apply to an entire organization or might be specific to a function, process, or production step.

Automotive Industry Action Group (AIAG): A global automotive trade association with about 1600 member companies that focuses on common business processes, implementation guidelines, education, and training.

Autonomation: A form of automation in which machinery automatically inspects each item after producing it and ceases production and notifies humans if a defect is detected. Toyota expanded the meaning of jidohka to include the responsibility of all workers to function similarly—to check every item produced and, if a defect is detected, make no more until the cause of the defect has been identified and corrected. Also see "jidohka."

Availability: The ability of a product to be in a state to perform its designated function under stated conditions at a given time.

Average chart: A control chart in which the subgroup average, X-bar, is used to evaluate the stability of the process level.

Average run lengths (ARL): On a control chart, the number of subgroups expected to be inspected before a shift in magnitude takes place.

Baka-yoke: A Japanese term for a manufacturing technique for preventing mistakes by designing the manufacturing process, equipment, and tools so an operation literally cannot be performed incorrectly. In addition to preventing incorrect operation, the technique usually provides a warning signal of some sort for incorrect performance. Also see "poka-yoke."

Balanced plant: A plant in which the capacity of all resources is balanced exactly with market demand.

Balanced scorecard: A management system that provides feedback on both internal business processes and external outcomes to continuously improve strategic performance and results.

Balancing the line: The process of evenly distributing both the quantity and variety of work across available work time, avoiding overburden, and underuse of resources. This eliminates bottlenecks and downtime, which translates into shorter flow time.

Baldrige award: See "Malcolm Baldrige National Quality Award."

Baseline measurement: The beginning point, based on an evaluation of output over a period of time, used to determine the process parameters prior to any improvement effort; the basis against which change is measured.

Batch and queue: Producing more than one piece and then moving the pieces to the next operation before they are needed.

Benchmarking: A technique in which a company measures its performance against that of best in class companies, determines how those companies achieved their performance levels, and uses the information to improve its own performance. Subjects that can be benchmarked include strategies, operations, and processes.

Best practice: A superior method or innovative practice that contributes to the improved performance of an organization, usually recognized as best by other peer organizations.

Big Q, little q: A term used to contrast the difference between managing for quality in all business processes and products (big Q) and managing for quality in a limited capacity—traditionally only in factory products and processes (little q).

Black Belt (BB): A full-time team leader responsible for implementing process improvement projects—define, measure, analyze, improve, and control (DMAIC) or define, measure, analyze, design, and verify (DMADV)—within a business to drive up customer satisfaction and productivity levels.

Blemish: An imperfection severe enough to be noticed but that should not cause any real impairment with respect to intended normal or reasonably foreseeable use. Also see "defect," "imperfection," and "nonconformity."

Block diagram: A diagram that shows the operation, interrelationships, and interdependencies of components in a system. Boxes, or blocks (hence the name), represent the components; connecting lines between the blocks represent interfaces. There are two types of block diagrams: a functional block diagram, which shows a system's subsystems and lower level products and their interrelationships and which interfaces with other systems; and a reliability block diagram, which is similar to the functional block diagram but is modified to emphasize those aspects influencing reliability.

Bottleneck: Any resource whose capacity is equal to or less than the demand placed on it.

Brainstorming: A technique teams use to generate ideas on a particular subject. Each person on the team is asked to think creatively and write down as many ideas as possible. The ideas are not discussed or reviewed until after the brainstorming session.

Breakthrough improvement: A dynamic, decisive movement to a new, higher level of performance.

c **Chart:** See "count chart."

Calibration: The comparison of a measurement instrument or system of unverified accuracy to a measurement instrument or system of known accuracy to detect any variation from the required performance specification.

Capability: The total range of inherent variation in a stable process determined by using data from control charts.

Capacity constraint resources: A series of nonbottlenecks (based on the sequence in which jobs are performed) that can act as a constraint.

Cascading: The continuing flow of the quality message down to, not through, the next level of supervision until it reaches all workers. Also see "deployment."

Cause: An identified reason for the presence of a defect or problem.

Cause and effect diagram: A tool for analyzing process dispersion. It is also referred to as the "Ishikawa diagram," because Kaoru Ishikawa developed it, and the "fishbone diagram," because the complete diagram resembles a fish skeleton. The diagram illustrates the main causes and subcauses leading to an effect (symptom). The cause and effect diagram is one of the "seven tools of quality" (see listing).

Cell: An arrangement of people, machines, materials, and equipment in which the processing steps are placed next to each other in sequential order and through which parts are processed in a continuous flow. The most common cell layout is a U shape.

Cellular manufacturing: Arranging machines in the correct process sequence, with operators remaining within the cell and materials presented to them from outside.

Centerline: A line on a graph that represents the overall average (mean) operating level of the process.

Certification: The result of a person meeting the established criteria set by a certificate granting organization.

Champion: A business leader or senior manager who ensures resources are available for training and projects, and who is involved in periodic project reviews; also an executive who supports and addresses Six Sigma organizational issues.

Change agent: An individual from within or outside an organization who facilitates change in the organization; might be the initiator of the change effort, but not necessarily.

Changeover: A process in which a production device is assigned to perform a different operation or a machine is set up to make a different part—for example, a new plastic resin and new mold in an injection molding machine.

Changeover time: The time required to modify a system or workstation, usually including both teardown time for the existing condition and setup time for the new condition.

Characteristic: The factors, elements, or measures that define and differentiate a process, function, product, service, or other entity.

Chart: A tool for organizing, summarizing, and depicting data in graphic form.

Charter: A written commitment approved by management stating the scope of authority for an improvement project or team.

Checklist: A tool for ensuring all important steps or actions in an operation has been taken. Checklists contain items important or relevant to an issue or situation. Checklists are often confused with check sheets (see listing).

Check sheet: A simple data recording device. The check sheet is custom designed by the user, which allows him or her to readily interpret the results. The check sheet is one of the "seven tools of quality" (see listing). Check sheets are often confused with checklists (see listing).

Common causes: The causes of variation that are inherent in a process over time. They affect every outcome of the process and everyone working in the process. Also see "special causes."

Complaint tracking: Collecting data, disseminating them to appropriate persons for resolution, monitoring complaint resolution progress, and communicating results.

Compliance: The state of an organization that meets prescribed specifications, contract terms, regulations, or standards.

Conformance: An affirmative indication or judgment that a product or service has met the requirements of a relevant specification, contract, or regulation.

Conformity assessment: All activities concerned with determining that relevant requirements in standards or regulations are fulfilled, including sampling, testing, inspection, certification, management system assessment, and registration, accreditation of the competence of those activities and recognition of an accreditation program's capability.

Constraints management: See "theory of constraints."

Consultant: An individual who has experience and expertise in applying tools and techniques to resolve process problems and who can advise and facilitate an organization's improvement efforts.

Consumer: The external customer to whom a product or service is ultimately delivered; also called end user.

Continuous flow production: A method in which items are produced and moved from one processing step to the next, one piece at a time. Each process makes only the one piece that the next process needs, and the transfer batch size is one. Also referred to as one-piece flow and single-piece flow.

Continuous improvement (CI): Sometimes called continual improvement. The ongoing improvement of products, services, or processes through incremental and breakthrough improvements.

Continuous quality improvement (CQI): A philosophy and attitude for analyzing capabilities and processes and improving them repeatedly to achieve customer satisfaction.

Control chart: A chart with upper and lower control limits on which values of some statistical measure for a series of samples or subgroups are plotted. The chart frequently shows a central line to help detect a trend of plotted values toward either control limit.

Control limits: The natural boundaries of a process within specified confidence levels, expressed as the upper control limit (UCL) and the lower control limit (LCL).

Control plan (CP): The written descriptions of the systems for controlling part and process quality by addressing the key characteristics and engineering requirements.

Corrective action: A solution meant to reduce or eliminate an identified problem.

Corrective action recommendation (CAR): The full cycle corrective action tool that offers ease and simplicity for employee involvement in the corrective action/process improvement cycle.

Cost of poor quality (COPQ): The costs associated with providing poor quality products or services. There are four categories: internal failure costs (costs associated with defects found before the customer receives the product or service), external failure costs (costs associated with defects found after the customer receives the product or service), appraisal costs (costs incurred to determine the degree of conformance to quality requirements), and prevention costs (costs incurred to keep failure and appraisal costs to a minimum).

Cost of quality (COQ): Another term for COPQ. It is considered by some to be synonymous with COPQ but is considered by others to be unique. While the two concepts emphasize the same ideas, some disagree as to which concept came first and which categories are included in each.

Count chart: A control chart for evaluating the stability of a process in terms of the count of events of a given classification occurring in a sample, known as a "*c*-chart."

Count per unit chart: A control chart for evaluating the stability of a process in terms of the average count of events of a given classification per unit occurring in a sample.

C_p**:** The ratio of tolerance to Six Sigma, or the upper specification limit (USL) minus the lower specification limit (LSL) divided by Six Sigma. It is sometimes referred to as the engineering tolerance divided by the natural tolerance and is only a measure of dispersion.

C_{pk} **index:** Equals the lesser of the USL minus the mean divided by Three Sigma (or the mean) minus the LSL divided by Three Sigma. The greater the C_{pk} value, the better.

Cross functional: A term used to describe a process or an activity that crosses the boundary between functions. A cross functional team consists of individuals from more than one organizational unit or function.

Customer: See "external customer" and "internal customer."

Customer delight: The result of delivering a product or service that exceeds customer expectations.

Customer satisfaction: The result of delivering a product or service that meets customer requirements.

Cycle: A sequence of operations repeated regularly.

Cycle time: The time required to complete one cycle of an operation. If cycle time for every operation in a complete process can be reduced to equal takt time, products can be made in single-piece flow. Also see "takt time."

Data: A set of collected facts. There are two basic kinds of numerical data: measured or variable data, such as "16 ounces," "4 miles," and "0.75 inches"; and counted or attribute data, such as "162 defects."

Decision matrix: A matrix teams use to evaluate problems or possible solutions. For example, a team might draw a matrix to evaluate possible solutions, listing them in the far left vertical column. Next, the team selects criteria to rate the possible solutions, writing them across the top row. Then, each possible solution is rated on a scale of 1–5 for each criterion, and the rating is recorded in the corresponding grid. Finally, the ratings of all the criteria for each possible solution are added to determine its total score. The total score is then used to help decide which solution deserves the most attention.

Defect: A product's or service's nonfulfillment of an intended requirement or reasonable expectation for use, including safety considerations. There are four classes of defects: class 1, very serious, leads directly to severe injury or catastrophic economic loss; class 2, serious, leads directly to significant injury or significant economic loss; class 3, major, is related to major problems with respect to intended normal or reasonably foreseeable use; and class 4, minor, is related to minor problems with respect to intended normal or reasonably foreseeable use. Also see "blemish," "imperfection," and "nonconformity."

Defective: A defective unit; a unit of product that contains one or more defects with respect to the quality characteristic(s) under consideration.

Delighter: A feature of a product or service that a customer does not expect to receive, but that gives pleasure to the customer when received. Also called an "exciter."

Deming cycle: Another term for the plan-do-study-act cycle. Walter Shewhart created it (calling it the plan-do-check-act cycle), but W. Edwards Deming popularized it, calling it plan-do-study-act. Also see "plan-do-check-act cycle."

Deployment: Dispersion, dissemination, broadcasting, or spreading communication throughout an organization, downward and laterally. Also see "cascading."

Deviation: In numerical data sets, the difference or distance of an individual observation or data value from the center point (often the mean) of the set distribution.

Dissatisfiers: The features or functions a customer expects that either are not present or are present but not adequate; also pertains to employees' expectations. Distribution (statistical): The amount of potential variation in the outputs of a process, typically expressed by its shape, average or standard deviation.

DMAIC: A data driven quality strategy for improving processes and an integral part of a Six Sigma quality initiative. DMAIC is an acronym for define, measure, analyze, improve, and control.

Effect: The result of an action being taken; the expected or predicted impact when an action is to be taken or is proposed.

Effectiveness: The state of having produced a decided on or desired effect.

Efficiency: The ratio of the output to the total input in a process.

Efficient: A term describing a process that operates effectively while consuming minimal resources (such as labor and time).

Eight wastes: Taiichi Ohno originally enumerated seven wastes (muda) and later added underutilized people as the eighth waste commonly found in physical production. The eight are: (1) overproduction ahead of demand; (2) waiting for the next process, worker, material, or equipment; (3) unnecessary transport of materials (for example, between functional areas of facilities, or to or from a stockroom or warehouse); (4) over-processing of parts due to poor tool and product design; (5) inventories more than the absolute minimum; (6) unnecessary movement by employees during the course of their work (such as to look for parts, tools, prints, or help); (7) production of defective parts; and (8) under-utilization of employees' brainpower, skills, experience, and talents.

EN 9100: An international quality management standard for the aerospace industry (see AS9100).

End user: See "consumer."

Error detection: A hybrid form of error proofing. It means a bad part can be made but will be caught immediately, and corrective action will be taken to prevent another bad part from being produced. A device is used to detect and stop the process when a bad part is made. This is used when error proofing is too expensive or not easily implemented.

Error proofing: The use of process or design features to prevent the acceptance or further processing of nonconforming products. Also known as "mistake proofing."

Exciter: See "delighter."

Expectations: Customer perceptions about how an organization's products and services will meet their specific needs and requirements.

External customer: A person or organization that receives a product, service, or information but is not part of the organization supplying it. Also see "internal customer."

External failure: Nonconformance identified by the external customers.

Failure: The inability of an item, product, or service to perform required functions on demand due to one or more defects.

Failure cost: The cost resulting from the occurrence of defects. One element of cost of quality or cost of poor quality.

Failure mode effects analysis (FMEA): A systematized group of activities to recognize and evaluate the potential failure of a product or process and its effects, identify actions that could eliminate or reduce the occurrence of the potential failure and document the process.

First in, first out (FIFO): The use of material produced by one process in the same order by the next process. A FIFO queue is filled by the supplying process and emptied by the customer process. When a FIFO lane gets full, production is stopped until the next (internal) customer has used some of that inventory.

Fishbone diagram: See "cause and effect diagram."

Fitness for use: A term used to indicate that a product or service fits the customer's defined purpose for that product or service.

Five S's (5S): Five Japanese terms beginning with "S" used to create a workplace suited for visual control and lean production. Seiri means to separate needed tools, parts, and instructions from unneeded materials and to remove the unneeded ones. Seiton means to neatly arrange and identify parts and tools for ease of use. Seiso means to conduct a cleanup campaign. Seiketsu means to conduct seiri, seiton, and seiso daily to maintain a workplace in perfect condition. Shitsuke means to form the habit of always following the first four S's.

Five whys: A technique for discovering the root causes of a problem and showing the relationship of causes by repeatedly asking the question, "Why?"

Flow: The progressive achievement of tasks along the value stream so a product proceeds from design to launch, order to delivery, and raw to finished materials in the hands of the customer with no stoppages, scrap, or backflows.

Flowchart: A graphical representation of the steps in a process. Flowcharts are drawn to better understand processes. One of the "seven tools of quality" (see listing).

Flow kaizen: Radical improvement, usually applied only once within a value stream.

Gage repeatability and reproducibility (GR&R): The evaluation of a gauging instrument's accuracy by determining whether its measurements are repeatable (there is close agreement among a number of consecutive measurements of the output for the same value of the input under the same operating conditions) and reproducible (there is close agreement among repeated measurements of the output for the same value of input made under the same operating conditions over a period of time).

Gap analysis: The comparison of a current condition to the desired state.

Goal: A broad statement describing a desired future condition or achievement without being specific about how much and when.

Go/no-go: State of a unit or product. Two parameters are possible: go (conforms to specifications) and no-go (does not conform to specifications).

Green Belt (GB): An employee who has been trained in the Six Sigma improvement method and will lead a process improvement or quality improvement team as part of his or her full-time job.

Heijunka: A method of leveling production, usually at the final assembly line, that makes just-in-time production possible. It involves averaging both the volume and sequence of different model types on a mixed model production line. Using this method avoids excessive batching of different types of product and volume fluctuations in the same product. Also see "production smoothing."

Histogram: A graphic summary of variation in a set of data. The pictorial nature of a histogram lets people see patterns that are difficult to detect in a simple table of numbers. One of the "seven tools of quality" (see listing).

Hoshin kanri: The selection of goals, projects to achieve the goals, designation of people and resources for project completion and establishment of project metrics. Also see "policy deployment."

Hoshin planning: A breakthrough planning. A Japanese strategic planning process in which a company develops up to four vision statements that indicate where the company should be in the next 5 years. Company goals and work plans are developed based on the vision statements. Periodic submitted audits are then conducted to monitor progress. Also see "value stream."

House of quality: A product planning matrix, somewhat resembling a house, which is developed during quality function deployment and shows the relationship of customer requirements to the means of achieving these requirements.

Imperfection: A quality characteristic's departure from its intended level or state without any association to conformance to specification requirements or to the usability of a product or service. Also see "blemish," "defect," and "nonconformity."

Improvement: The positive effect of a process change effort.

In-control process: A process in which the statistical measure being evaluated is in a state of statistical control; in other words, the variations among the observed sampling results can be attributed to a constant system of chance causes. Also see "out-of-control process."

Incremental improvement: Improvement implemented on a continual basis.

Indicators: Established measures to determine how well an organization is meeting its customers' needs and other operational and financial performance expectations.

Inputs: The products, services, and material obtained from suppliers to produce the outputs delivered to customers.

Inspection: Measuring, examining, testing, and gauging one or more characteristics of a product or service and comparing the results with specified requirements to determine whether conformity is achieved for each characteristic.

Inspection cost: The cost associated with inspecting a product to ensure it meets the internal or external customer's needs and requirements; an appraisal cost.

Inspection, 100%: The inspection of all the units in the lot or batch.

Internal customer: The recipient (person or department) within an organization of another person's or department's output (product, service or information). Also see "external customer."

Internal failure: A product failure that occurs before the product is delivered to external customers.

International Organization for Standardization: A network of national standards institutes from 157 countries working in partnership with international organizations, governments, industry, business, and consumer representatives to develop and publish international standards; acts as a bridge between public and private sectors.

Interrelationship diagram: A management tool that depicts the relationship among factors in a complex situation, also called "relations diagram."

Inventory: In lean, the money invested to purchase things an organization intends to sell.

Ishikawa diagram: See "cause and effect diagram."

ISO 14000: An environmental management standard related to what organizations do that affects their physical surroundings.

ISO 9000 series standards: A set of international standards on quality management and quality assurance developed to help companies effectively document the quality system elements to be implemented to maintain an efficient quality system. The standards, initially published in 1987, are not specific to any particular industry, product, or service. The standards were developed by the International Organization for Standardization (see listing). The standards underwent major revision in 2000 and now include ISO 9000:2005 (definitions), ISO 9001:2008 (requirements), and ISO 9004:2009 (continuous improvement).

ISO/TS 16949: International Organization for Standardization international technical specification for quality management systems, with particular requirements for the application of ISO 9001:2008 for automotive production and relevant service part organization, generally replaced the U.S. QS-9000 standard. Now in its second edition.

Jidohka: Stopping a line automatically when a defective part is detected. Any necessary improvements can then be made by directing attention to the stopped equipment and the worker who stopped the operation. The jidohka system puts faith in the worker as a thinker and allows all workers the right to stop the line on which they are working. Also see "autonomation."

Job instruction: A quality system documentation that describes work conducted in one function in a company, such as setup, inspection, rework, or operator.

Just-in-time (JIT) manufacturing: An optimal material requirement planning system for a manufacturing process in which there is little or no manufacturing material inventory on hand at the manufacturing site and little or no incoming inspection.

Kaizen: A Japanese term that means gradual unending improvement by doing little things better and setting and achieving increasingly higher standards. Masaaki Imai made the term famous in his book, *Kaizen: The Key to Japan's Competitive Success.*

Kanban: A Japanese term for one of the primary tools of a just-in-time system. It maintains an orderly and efficient flow of materials throughout the entire manufacturing process. It is usually a printed card that contains specific information such as part name, description, and quantity.

Key performance indicator (KPI): A statistical measure of how well an organization is doing in a particular area. A KPI could measure a company's financial performance or how it is holding up against customer requirements.

Laboratory: A test facility that can include chemical, metallurgical, dimensional, physical, electrical, and reliability testing, or test validation.

Lead time: The total time a customer must wait to receive a product after placing an order.

Leadership: An essential part of a quality improvement effort. The organization leaders must establish a vision, communicate that vision to those in the organization, and provide the tools and knowledge necessary to accomplish the vision.

Lean: Producing the maximum sellable products or services at the lowest operational cost while optimizing inventory levels.

Lean enterprise: A manufacturing company organized to eliminate all unproductive effort and unnecessary investment, both on the shop floor and in office functions.

Lean manufacturing/production: An initiative focused on eliminating all waste in manufacturing processes. Principles of lean manufacturing include zero waiting time, zero inventory, scheduling (internal customer pull instead of push system), batch to flow (cut batch sizes), line balancing, and cutting actual process times. The production systems are characterized by optimum automation, just-in-time supplier delivery disciplines, quick changeover times, high levels of quality, and continuous improvement.

Lean migration: The journey from traditional manufacturing methods to one in which all forms of waste are systematically eliminated.

Lower control limit (LCL): Control limit for points below the central line in a control chart.

Management review: A periodic management meeting to review the status and effectiveness of the organization's quality management system.

Manager: An individual charged with managing resources and processes.

Master Black Belt (MBB): A Six Sigma or quality expert responsible for strategic implementations in an organization. An MBB is qualified to teach other Six Sigma facilitators the methods, tools, and applications in all functions and levels of the company and is a resource for using statistical process control in processes.

Material handling: The methods, equipment, and systems for conveying materials to various machines and processing areas and for transferring finished parts to assembly, packaging, and shipping areas.

Matrix: A planning tool for displaying the relationships among various data sets.

Mean: A measure of central tendency; the arithmetic average of all measurements in a data set.

Measure: The criteria, metric, or means to which a comparison is made with output.

Measurement: The act or process of quantitatively comparing results with requirements.

Measurement system: All operations, procedures, devices, and other equipment or personnel used to assign a value to the characteristic being measured.

Measurement uncertainty: The result of random effects and imperfect correction of systemic effects in obtaining a measurement value that result in variation from the actual true value; also known as measurement error.

Median: The middle number or center value of a set of data in which all the data are arranged in sequence.

Metric: A standard for measurement.

Metrology: The science of weights and measures or of measurement; a system of weights and measures.

Mission: An organization's purpose.

Mistake proofing: The use of production or design features to prevent the manufacture or passing downstream a nonconforming product; also known as "error proofing."

Muda: Japanese for waste; any activity that consumes resources but creates no value for the customer.

n: The number of units in a sample.

N: The number of units in a population.

National Institute of Standards and Technology (NIST): An agency of the U.S. Department of Commerce that develops and promotes measurements, standards, and technology and manages the Malcolm Baldrige National Quality Award.

Next operation as customer: The concept of internal customers in which every operation is both a receiver and a provider.

Nonconforming record (NCR): A permanent record—made in writing—for accounting and preserving the knowledge of a nonconforming condition for the purposes of documenting facts or events.

Nonconformity: The nonfulfillment of a specified requirement. Also see "blemish," "defect," and "imperfection."

Objective: A specific statement of a desired short-term condition or achievement includes measurable end results to be accomplished by specific teams or individuals within time limits.

One-piece flow: The opposite of batch and queue; instead of building many products and then holding them in line for the next step in the process, products go through each step in the process one at a time, without interruption. Meant to improve quality and lower costs.

One-touch exchange of dies: The reduction of die setup to a single step. Also see "single-minute."

Operations: The work or steps to transform raw materials to finished product.

Out-of-control process: A process in which the statistical measure being evaluated is not in a state of statistical control. In other words, the variations among the observed sampling results cannot be attributed to a constant system of chance causes. Also see "in-control process."

Out of spec: A term that indicates a unit does not meet a given requirement or specification.

Outputs: The products, materials, services, or information provided to customers (internal or external), from a process.

Painted floor: A lean manufacturing technique to provide visual indications to determine stock levels. Similar to kanban.

Pareto chart: A graphical tool for ranking causes from most significant to least significant. It is based on the Pareto principle, which was first defined by Joseph M. Juran in 1950. The principle, named after nineteenth century economist Vilfredo Pareto, suggests most effects come from relatively few causes; that is, 80% of the effects come from 20% of the possible causes. One of the "seven tools of qualities" (see listing).

p Chart: See "percent chart."

PDCA cycle: See "plan-do-check-act cycle."

Percent chart: A control chart for evaluating the stability of a process in terms of the percentage of the total number of units in a sample in which an event of a given classification occurs. Also referred to as a proportion chart.

Plan-do-check-act (PDCA) cycle: A four-step process for quality improvement. In the first step (plan), a way to effect improvement is developed. In the second step (do), the plan is carried out, preferably on a small scale. In the third step (check), a study takes place between what was predicted and what was observed in the previous step. In the last step (act), action is taken on the causal system to effect the desired change. The plan-do-check-act cycle is sometimes referred to as the Shewhart cycle, because Walter A. Shewhart discussed the concept in his book *Statistical Method from the Viewpoint of Quality Control*, and as the Deming cycle, because W. Edwards Deming introduced the concept in Japan. The Japanese subsequently called it the Deming cycle. Also called the plan-do-study-act (PDSA) cycle.

Poka-yoke: Japanese term that means mistake proofing. A poka-yoke device is one that prevents incorrect parts from being made or assembled or easily identifies a flaw or error.

Policy: An overarching plan (direction) for achieving an organization's goals.

Policy deployment: The selection of goals and projects to achieve the goals, designation of people, and resources for project completion and establishment of project metrics. Also see "hoshin kanri."

Precision: The aspect of measurement that addresses repeatability or consistency when an identical item is measured several times.

Preventive action: Action taken to remove or improve a process to prevent potential future occurrences of a nonconformance.

Prevention cost: The cost incurred by actions taken to prevent a nonconformance from occurring; one element of cost of quality or cost of poor quality.

Prevention versus detection: A term used to contrast two types of quality activities. Prevention refers to activities for preventing nonconformances in products and services. Detection refers to activities for detecting nonconformances already in products and services. Another phrase to describe this distinction is "designing in quality versus inspecting in quality."

Procedure: The steps in a process and how these steps are to be performed for the process to fulfill a customer's requirements; usually documented.

Process: A set of interrelated work activities characterized by a set of specific inputs and value added tasks that make up a procedure for a set of specific outputs.

Process capability: A statistical measure of the inherent process variability of a given characteristic. The most widely accepted formula for process capability is Six Sigma.

Process capability index: The value of the tolerance specified for the characteristic divided by the process capability. The several types of process capability indexes include the widely used C_{pk} and C_p.

Process control: The method for keeping a process within boundaries; the act of minimizing the variation of a process.

Process improvement: The application of the plan-do-check-act cycle (see listing) to processes to produce positive improvement and better meet the needs and expectations of customers.

Process improvement team: A structured group often made up of cross functional members who work together to improve a process or processes.

Process owner: The person who coordinates the various functions and work activities at all levels of a process has the authority or ability to make changes in the process as required and manages the entire process cycle to ensure performance effectiveness.

Process quality: The value of percentage defective or of defects per hundred units in product from a given process. *Note*: The symbols "p" and "c" are commonly used to represent the true process average in fraction defective or defects per unit; and "$100p$" and "$100c$" the true process average in percentage defective or in defects per hundred units.

Production (analysis) board: A job site board on which hourly production targets are recorded, along with the actual production achieved. Details concerning problems and abnormal conditions are also recorded. Management checks the board hourly, takes steps to prevent recurrence of abnormalities, and confirms the positive effects of the job site improvements that have been made. An example of visual management.

Production part approval process (PPAP): A big three automotive process that defines the generic requirements for approval of production parts, including production and bulk materials. Its purpose is to determine during an actual production run at the quoted production rates whether all customer engineering design record and specification requirements are properly understood by the supplier and that the process has the potential to produce product consistently meeting these requirements.

Production smoothing: Keeping total manufacturing volume as constant as possible. Also see "heijunka."

Productivity: A measurement of output for a given amount of input.

Proportion chart: See "percent chart."

Pull system: An alternative to scheduling individual processes, in which the customer process withdraws the items it needs from a supermarket (see listing) and the supplying process produces to replenish what was withdrawn; used to avoid push. Also see "kanban."

Q9000 series: Refers to ANSI/ISO/ASQ Q9000 series of standards, which is the verbatim American adoption of the 2000 edition of the ISO 9000 series standards.

Quality: A subjective term for which each person or sector has its own definition. In technical usage, quality can have two meanings: (1) the characteristics of a product or service that bear on its ability to satisfy stated or implied needs and (2) a product or service free of deficiencies. According to Joseph Juran, quality means "fitness for use"; according to Philip Crosby, it means "conformance to requirements."

Quality assurance/quality control (QA/QC): Two terms that have many interpretations because of the multiple definitions for the words "assurance" and "control." For example, "assurance" can mean the act of giving confidence, the state of being certain, or the act of making certain; "control" can mean an evaluation to indicate needed corrective responses, the act of guiding or the state of a process in which the variability is attributable to a constant system of chance causes. (For a detailed discussion on the multiple definitions, see ANSI/ISO/ASQ A3534-2, Statistics—Vocabulary and Symbols—Statistical Quality Control.) One definition of quality assurance is all the planned and systematic activities implemented within the quality system that can be demonstrated to provide confidence that a product or service will fulfill requirements for quality. One definition for quality control is the operational techniques and activities used to fulfill requirements for quality. Often, however, "quality assurance" and "quality control" are used interchangeably, referring to the actions performed to ensure the quality of a product, service, or process.

Quality audit: A systematic, independent examination, and review to determine whether quality activities and related results comply with plans and whether these plans are implemented effectively and are suitable to achieve the objectives.

Quality circle: A quality improvement or self-improvement study group composed of a small number of employees (10 or fewer) and their supervisor. Quality circles originated in Japan, where they are called quality control circles.

Quality control: See "quality assurance/quality control."

Quality costs: See "cost of poor quality."

Quality engineering: The analysis of a manufacturing system at all stages to maximize the quality of the process itself and the products it produces.

Quality function deployment (QFD): A structured method in which customer requirements are translated into appropriate technical requirements for each stage of product development and production. The QFD process is often referred to as listening to the voice of the customer.

Quality management (QM): The application of a quality management system in managing a process to achieve maximum customer satisfaction at the lowest overall cost to the organization while continuing to improve the process.

Quality management system (QMS): A formalized system that documents the structure, responsibilities, and procedures required to achieve effective quality management.

Quality plan: A document or set of documents that describe the standards, quality practices, resources, and processes pertinent to a specific product, service, or project.

Quality policy: An organization's general statement of its beliefs about quality, how quality will come about, and its expected result.

Quality tool: An instrument or technique to support and improve the activities of process quality management and improvement.

Quality trilogy: A three-pronged approach to managing for quality. The three legs are quality planning (developing the products and processes required to meet customer needs), quality control (meeting product and process goals), and quality improvement (achieving unprecedented levels of performance).

Queue time: The time a product spends in a line awaiting the next design, order processing, or fabrication step.

Quick changeover: The ability to change tooling and fixtures rapidly (usually within minutes) so multiple products can be run on the same machine.

Random cause: A cause of variation due to chance and not assignable to any factor.

Range (statistical): The measure of dispersion in a data set (the difference between the highest and lowest values).

Range chart (*R* Chart): A control chart in which the subgroup range, R, evaluates the stability of the variability within a process.

Registrar: Generally accepted U.S. equivalent term for "certification body."

Registration: The act of including an organization, product, service, or process in a compilation of those having the same or similar attributes.

Registration to standards: A process in which an accredited, independent third-party organization conducts an on-site audit of a company's operations against the requirements of the standard to which the company wants to be registered. Upon successful completion of the audit, the company receives a certificate indicating it has met the standard requirements. In countries outside the United States, this is generally known as certification.

Repeatability: The variation in measurements obtained when one measurement device is used several times by the same person to measure the same characteristic on the same product.

Reproducibility: The variation in measurements made by different people using the same measuring device to measure the same characteristic on the same product.

Requirements: The ability of an item to perform a required function under stated conditions for a stated period of time.

Run chart: A chart showing a line connecting numerous data points collected from a process running over time.

Runner: A person on the production floor who paces the entire value stream through the pickup and delivery of materials through kanban (see listing) usage.

Sample standard deviation chart (*S* Chart): A control chart in which the subgroup standard deviation, S, is used to evaluate the stability of the variability within a process.

Sanitizing: English translation of seiso, one of the Japanese 5S's used for workplace organization. Sanitizing (also referred to as shining or sweeping) is the act of cleaning the work area. Dirt is often the root cause of premature equipment wear, safety problems, and defects.

Satisfier: A term used to describe the quality level received by a customer when a product or service meets expectations.

Scatter diagram: A graphical technique to analyze the relationship between two variables. Two sets of data are plotted on a graph, with the y-axis being used for the variable to be predicted and the x-axis being used for the variable to make the prediction. The graph will show possible relationships (although two variables might appear to be related, they might not be; those who know most about the variables must make that evaluation). One of the "seven tools of quality" (see listing).

Scorecard: An evaluation device, usually in the form of a questionnaire, that specifies the criteria customers will use to rate your business' performance in satisfying customer requirements.

Seven tools of quality: Tools that help organizations understand their processes to improve them. The tools are the cause and effect diagram, check sheet, control chart, flowchart, histogram, Pareto chart, and scatter diagram (see individual entries).

Seven wastes: See "eight wastes."

Shadow board: A visual management tool painted to indicate where tools belong and which tools are missing.

Shewhart cycle: See "plan-do-check-act cycle."

Sifting: English translation of Japanese seiri, one of the 5S's used for workplace organization. Sifting involves screening through unnecessary materials and simplifying the work environment. Sifting is separating the essential from the nonessential.

Sigma: One standard deviation in a normally distributed process.

Single-minute exchange of dies: A series of techniques pioneered by Shigeo Shingo for changeovers of production machinery in less than 10 minutes. The long-term objective is always zero setup, in which changeovers are instantaneous and do not interfere in any way with continuous flow. Setup in a single minute is not required, but used as a reference (see "one-touch exchange of dies," "internal setup," and "external setup").

Single-piece flow: A process in which products proceed, one complete product at a time, through various operations in design, order taking and production without interruptions, backflows or scrap.

Six Sigma: A method that provides organizations tools to improve the capability of their business processes. This increase in performance and decrease in process variation lead to defect reduction and improvement in profits, employee morale, and quality of products or services. Six Sigma quality is a term generally used to indicate a process is well controlled (±6 s from the centerline in a control chart).

Six Sigma quality: A term generally used to indicate process capability in terms of process spread measured by standard deviations in a normally distributed process.

Sort: English translation of the Japanese word seiri, one of the 5S's used for workplace organization. Sorting (also referred to as structuring or sifting) involves organizing essential materials. It helps the operator to find materials when needed.

Special causes: The causes of variation that arise because of special circumstances. They are not an inherent part of a process. Special causes are also referred to as assignable causes. Also see "common causes."

Special characteristic: Automotive ISO/TS 16949 term for key product or process characteristics.

Specification: A document that states the requirements to which a given product or service must conform.

Standard: The metric, specification, gage, statement, category, segment, grouping, behavior, event, or physical product sample against which the outputs of a process are compared and declared acceptable or unacceptable.

Standard deviation (statistical): A computed measure of variability indicating the spread of the data set around the mean.

Standard work: A precise description of each work activity, specifying cycle time, takt time, the work sequence of specific tasks, and the minimum inventory of parts on hand needed to conduct the activity. All jobs are organized around human motion to create an efficient sequence without waste. Work organized in such a way is called standard (ized) work. The three elements that make up standard work are takt time, working sequence, and standard in-process stock (see individual listings).

Standardization: When policies and common procedures are used to manage processes throughout the system. Also, English translation of the Japanese word seiketsu, one of the Japanese 5S's (see listing) used for workplace organization.

Statistical process control (SPC): The application of statistical techniques to control a process; often used interchangeably with the term "statistical quality control."

Stop the line authority: The power given to workers to stop the process when abnormalities occur, allowing them to prevent the defect or variation from being passed along.

Strategic planning: The process an organization uses to envision its future and develop the appropriate strategies, goals, objectives, and action plans.

Strengths, weaknesses, opportunities, threats (SWOT) analysis: A strategic technique used to assess what an organization is facing.

Stretch goals: A set of goals designed to position an organization to meet future requirements.

Structural variation: Variation caused by regular, systematic changes in output, such as seasonal patterns and long-term trends.

Suboptimization: A condition in which gains made in one activity are offset by losses in another activity or activities that are caused by the same actions that created gains in the first activity.

Supermarket: The storage locations of parts before they go on to the next operation. Supermarkets are managed by predetermined maximum and minimum inventory levels. Each item in the plant is at a designated location.

Supplier: A source of materials, service, or information input provided to a process.

Supplier quality assurance: The confidence that a supplier's product or service will fulfill its customers' needs. This confidence is achieved by creating a relationship between the customer and supplier that ensures the product will be fit for use with minimal corrective action and inspection. According to Joseph M. Juran, nine primary activities are needed: (1) define product and program quality requirements; (2) evaluate alternative suppliers; (3) select suppliers; (4) conduct joint quality planning; (5) cooperate with the supplier during the execution of the contract; (6) obtain proof of conformance to requirements; (7) certify qualified suppliers; (8) conduct quality improvement programs as required; and (9) create and use supplier quality ratings.

Supply chain: The series of suppliers to a given process.

Surveillance: The continual monitoring of a process; a type of periodic assessment or audit conducted to determine whether a process continues to perform to a predetermined standard.

Survey: The act of examining a process or questioning a selected sample of individuals to obtain data about a process, product, or service.

Sustain: The English translation of shitsuke, one of the 5S's (see listing) used for workplace organization. Sustaining (also referred to as self-disciplining) is the continuation of sorting, setting in order, and sanitizing. It addresses the need to perform the 5S's on an ongoing and systematic basis.

Symptom: An observable phenomenon arising from and accompanying a defect.

System: A group of interdependent processes and people that together perform a common mission.

System kaizen: An improvement aimed at an entire value stream.

Takt time: The rate of customer demand; takt time is calculated by dividing production time by the quantity of product the customer requires in that time. Takt is the heartbeat of a lean manufacturing system. Also see "cycle time."

Tampering: An action taken to compensate for variation within the control limits of a stable system; tampering increases rather than decreases variation, as evidenced in the funnel experiment.

Task: A specific, definable activity to perform an assigned piece of work often finished within a certain time.

TL 9000: A quality management standard for the telecommunications industry based on ISO 9000. Its purpose is to define the requirements for the design, development, production, delivery, installation, and maintenance of products and services. Included are cost and performance based measurements that measure reliability and quality performance of the products and services.

Tolerance: The maximum and minimum limit values a product can have and still meet customer requirements.

Top management commitment: The participation of the highest level officials in their organization's quality improvement efforts. Their participation includes establishing and serving on a quality committee, establishing quality policies and goals, deploying those goals to lower levels of the organization, providing the resources and training lower levels need to achieve the goals, participating in quality improvement teams, reviewing progress organization wide, recognizing those who have performed well and revising the current reward system to reflect the importance of achieving the quality goals.

Total quality: A strategic integrated system for achieving customer satisfaction that involves all managers and employees and uses quantitative methods to continuously improve an organization's processes.

Toyota production system (TPS): The production system developed by Toyota Motor Corp. to provide best quality, lowest cost, and shortest lead time through eliminating waste. TPS is based on two pillars: just-in-time and jidohka (see listings). TPS is maintained and improved through iterations of standardized work and kaizen (see listing.)

Tree diagram: A management tool that depicts the hierarchy of tasks and subtasks needed to complete an objective. The finished diagram bears a resemblance to a tree.

Trend: The graphical representation of a variable's tendency, over time, to increase, decrease, or remain unchanged.

Trend control chart: A control chart in which the deviation of the subgroup average, X-bar, from an expected trend in the process level is used to evaluate the stability of a process.

***u* Chart:** Count-per-unit chart.

Unit: An object for which a measurement or observation can be made; commonly used in the sense of a "unit of product," the entity of product inspected to determine whether it is defective or nondefective.

Upper control limit (UCL): Control limit for points above the central line in a control chart.

Validation: The act of confirming a product or service meets the requirements for which it was intended.

Validity: The ability of a feedback instrument to measure what it was intended to measure; also, the degree to which inferences derived from measurements are meaningful.

Value added: A term used to describe activities that transform input into a customer (internal or external) usable output.

Value analysis: Analyzing the value stream to identify value added and nonvalue-added activities.

Value stream: All activities, both value added and nonvalue added, required to bring a product from raw material state into the hands of the customer, bring a customer requirement from order to delivery and bring a design from concept to launch. Also see "information flow" and "hoshin planning."

Value stream mapping: A pencil and paper tool used in two stages. First, follow a product's production path from beginning to end and draw a visual representation of every process in the material and information flows. Second, draw a future state map of how value should flow. The most important map is the future state map.

Variable data: Measurement information. Control charts based on variable data include average ($\overline{X}$) chart, range (R) chart, and sample standard deviation (S) chart (see individual listings).

Variation: A change in data, characteristic, or function caused by one of four factors: special causes, common causes, tampering, or structural variation (see individual entries).

Verification: The act of determining whether products and services conform to specific requirements.

Vision: An overarching statement of the way an organization wants to be; an ideal state of being at a future point.

Visual controls: Any devices that help operators quickly and accurately gage production status at a glance. Progress indicators and problem indicators help assemblers see when production is ahead, behind, or on schedule. They allow everyone to instantly see the group's performance and increase the sense of ownership in the area. Also see "andon board," "kanban," "production board," "painted floor," and "shadow board."

Voice of the customer: The expressed requirements and expectations of customers relative to products or services, as documented and disseminated to the providing organization's members.

Waste: Any activity that consumes resources and produces no added value to the product or service a customer receives. Also known as muda.

Work in process: Items between machines or equipment waiting to be processed.

Working sequence: One of three elements of standard work; refers to the sequence of operations in a single process that leads a floor worker to most efficiently produce quality goods.

World-class quality: A term used to indicate a standard of excellence: best of the best.

$\bar{X}$ Chart: Average chart.

Zero defects: A performance standard and method Philip B. Crosby developed; states that if people commit themselves to watching details and avoiding errors, they can move closer to the goal of zero defects.

Index